STUDIES IN ENGLISH RELIGION
IN THE SEVENTEENTH CENTURY

STUDIES IN ENGLISH RELIGION IN THE SEVENTEENTH CENTURY

ST. MARGARET'S LECTURES

1903

By H. HENSLEY HENSON, B.D.

CANON OF WESTMINSTER AND RECTOR OF ST. MARGARET'S, WESTMINSTER
LATE FELLOW OF ALL SOULS' COLLEGE, OXFORD

WIPF & STOCK · Eugene, Oregon

Wipf and Stock Publishers
199 W 8th Ave, Suite 3
Eugene, OR 97401

Studies in English Religion in the Seventeenth Century
St. Margaret Lectures, 1903
By Henson, H. Hensley
ISBN 13: 978-1-62564-712-2
Publication date 2/18/2014
Previously published by E. P. Dutton, 1903

TO THE WARDEN AND FELLOWS OF
ALL SOULS' COLLEGE, OXFORD
IN GRATEFUL MEMORY OF
THEIR KINDNESS AND CONFIDENCE
CONTINUED THROUGH NINETEEN YEARS
(1884–1903)
THE AUTHOR INSCRIBES
THIS VOLUME
WITH THE UTMOST AFFECTION

Preface

SOME years ago I formed the design of writing a history of the "Savoy Conference," and, by way of preparing myself for my task, I directed my reading to the literature of the seventeenth century. In the summer of 1900 I printed for private circulation two lectures, the one on "The religious situation under Elizabeth," the other on "The Hampton Court Conference," and these lectures were republished last year, together with other essays, in a volume entitled *Cross-bench Views of Current Church Questions*. When, in the course of my duty, I had to arrange for a fresh series of S. Margaret's Lectures, many persons expressed to me their desire that I should take the opportunity of continuing my discussion of English religion in the seventeenth century. That will, perhaps, suffice to explain the subject of the lectures for 1903, and the fact that I myself was the lecturer. In adopting the title "studies," I could not escape from the limitations implied in the composition of lectures intended in the first instance for delivery in a church. A few leading truths insisted upon again and again, a few representative facts discussed with care, a few authorities advanced and used throughout—these would seem to be the unavoidable features of public lectures, designed to set out clearly positions, deliberately adopted, which, for their sufficient establishing, would properly demand a more elaborate treatment. The service which such "studies" are able to render is that of suggesting points of view and stimulating thought. Incidentally they may contribute information, but that is not their proper work. If I insist upon the limitations under which I have perforce laboured, it is in order to protect myself against a kind of criticism which, however legitimate in other spheres, is out of place in connection with these lectures. It is not to be inferred that unnamed authorities are also unknown and unused, or that important facts unmentioned are also unconsidered. Much had to be taken for granted as already known, and it seemed to me that this might be the more reasonably done since the period of history dealt with has been, perhaps, more thoroughly and effectively handled in easily accessible works than any other. The time has not come yet, if it ever comes, when such books as Dr. Masson's *Life of John Milton*, and Dr. Gardiner's great *History of England from the Accession of James I.* will need to be rewritten.

Of Dr. Gardiner, indeed, it is impossible for any student of history to speak without indulging in the language of genuine admiration. Nothing seems to have escaped his notice; nothing was able to deflect his judgment. He moved amid the bewildering controversies of the most controversial of centuries with a firm and even step, and, almost alone among the historians of that age, he has dealt equal justice to the protagonists of the conflicting causes, which stir men's hearts still and still inflame their passions. Charles, Laud, and Strafford are seen at their best on those pages which yet record with luminous sympathy the exploits of Pym, Owen, and Oliver; for the author had an intuitive appreciation of the higher elements in them all, and was able to divine and utter their often half-understood and clumsily-expressed ideals, as partisans then and apologists now, can never do. The very spirit of historic science inspires the calm and lucid narrative and the balanced judgment of Samuel Rawson Gardiner. It is impossible not to compare him advantageously in these respects with his great precursor in the study of the seventeenth century, Lord Macaulay. In another respect the two historians may be compared. Lord Macaulay lies buried in Poets' Corner, and few graves in that venerable place attract more general homage; but neither in Westminster Abbey, the treasure-house of national distinction, nor in S. Margaret's, the home of Parliamentary traditions, is there any memorial of one who was not only the historian of the most famous Parliament that has ever sat at Westminster, but also the most laborious, devoted, and disinterested of all the students of our national past. It may be fairly questioned whether Dr. Gardiner's historical writings do not constitute the greatest single achievement of the nineteenth century in the sphere of English historical work.

In the account of Presbyterianism in England I must acknowledge with special gratitude the help I have received from Mr. William A. Shaw's careful and valuable *History of the English Church during the Civil Wars and under the Commonwealth*, 1640-1660. Other acknowledgments have, I think, been made where they are required; but, mainly, I have not concerned myself with modern writers, preferring to draw what I had to say from the men of the time, and base my contentions on their evidence.

I have more frequently quoted from the voluminous writings of Richard Baxter than from any other contemporary, and I did so with the deliberate design of bringing once more into prominence the somewhat forgotten merits of that admirable man. It is much to be desired that some competent scholar would undertake the publication of a new edition of the *Reliquiae Baxterianae*. Matthew Sylvester, the original editor, was wholly without qualifications for his task, and he has given to us one of the most interesting and valuable autobiographies in the language in a state of such confusion, so swollen with documents, and destitute of notes of time, and other indispensable aids to the reader, that it is certainly the case that, outside the coteries of avowed historians, this work is only known by a few extracts. If the documents were removed from the text to an appendix, the text itself broken up into chapters or sections, and the whole carefully edited with explanatory notes, the *Reliquiae Baxterianae* would take rank at once as a book indispensable for students of the seventeenth century, and worthy of a place alongside the best literary productions of the time.

The seventeenth century was perhaps the most theological of all historic epochs, for it may be doubted whether the popular discussions of technical theology which Socrates describes as prevailing in the Nicene age really indicated any general dominance of theology in the region of popular practice, and in the "Ages of Faith" the intelligence of the average multitude slumbered under the unquestioned empire of the Church. And because the age was thus pre-eminently theological, it presented everywhere the strangest paradoxes. It is hard for the modern student to combine in a single view the barbarous superstition which gave a career to the miscreant Hopkins, famous as "the Witchfinder," and the pure and reasonable religion of such men as Baxter or Jeremy Taylor, or (which is still more perplexing) to understand in such men the coexistence of the manliest thinking and the worthiest living with the most infantile credulity. But this paradoxical age, when theology was not merely still, in the general estimate, the *summa scientiarum*, but even had passed into the political sphere and seized on the helm of government, stands in direct and intimate connection with our own time, the least theological and, perhaps, the least superstitious of all times. It is to the seventeenth century that the politician and the constitutional lawyer refer for the decisive events out of which the British Constitution finally emerged. As with the State so with the Church. The seventeenth century determined the singular religious constitution of the British people. Then the two established Churches received their present form, and then, not less, the great Nonconformist denominations took shape. While, however, there has passed upon the social and intellectual conditions of the country an immense revolution, and while political institutions have steadily developed along the lines laid down at the end of the seventeenth century, in the department of the Churches there has been a rigidity, equally irrational and unfortunate. The practical system, established in canons and rubrics, has indeed fallen everywhere into desuetude, for the habits of the modern community are not patient of it, and against national habits the best-considered and most authoritative systems of discipline are wholly incapable of enforcement, but the ecclesiastical system in the more limited sense remains still operative. The worship and formal belief of the established Churches are still determined by the decisions of the seventeenth century. The Act of Uniformity passed at the Restoration, under circumstances the least favourable in the world to the creation of a lasting "settlement," remains binding still on the Church of England, and constitutes the most formidable legal barrier to healthy ecclesiastical development. That calamitous measure belongs historically to the statutes of the Caroline Penal Code, of which it is now the solitary survivor, and so long as it remains on the statute-book the National Church is, in certain important directions, unable to advance or develop.

But not only in the region of ecclesiastical politics is the influence of the seventeenth century thus direct and considerable: in the wider religious life of the nation that influence is hardly less. The religious public still concerns itself with the issues which divided men two centuries and more ago, and the old confusions of thought and violences of fanaticism tend, under the milder conditions which now obtain, to repeat themselves. It follows, therefore, that for the right understanding of contemporary controversies and the just handling of practical problems of our own time a knowledge of the seventeenth century is eminently requisite. And such knowledge is, for the most part, not very accessible. The general histories are good, but they naturally concern themselves mainly with the secular aspect; the religious histories are almost invariably written from a partisan standpoint. Moreover the mass of events and characters is so great that there is always the danger of losing the just sense of proportion.

Such considerations seemed to recommend the plan of such a volume as this, in which, while no attempt is made to write a complete or continuous history, certain subjects of critical importance or exceptional intrinsic interest are selected and treated with sufficient care to indicate their permanent bearings. Such a volume, if it gain the object with which it was designed, would be a serviceable introduction to more detailed study of the period, and might tend to rectify the mental perspective of those students of English ecclesiastical history who have had the misfortune of reading the past through the coloured glasses of religious party.

It would be affectation to deny that I was influenced in the choice of the subjects of these studies by contemporary events, which have brought again into prominence among us the very issues which perplexed and divided our ancestors more than two centuries since. Nor am I wholly without hope that by pointing men to the historic causes of their religious conflicts I may, in however humble a degree, be serving the interest of that pacification which thoughtful persons are everywhere coming to desire.

H. HENSLEY HENSON

August, 1903

Contents

	PAGE
THE PRÆ-LAUDIAN CHURCH OF ENGLAND	1
SABBATARIANISM	35
THE PRESBYTERIAN EXPERIMENT	76
ERASTIANISM	125
CASUISTRY	171
TOLERATION	211

The Præ-Laudian Church

It is recognised on all hands that Archbishop Laud stands in the history of the Anglican Church for something more than a powerful and prominent individual. He represented a movement and expressed a tendency; he was the martyr of a cause and the prophet of a change. The ecclesiastical settlement of the Restoration was inspired by the principles, and, in some sense, realised the ideals of the party, which seemed to have perished when the Archbishop laid his head on the block. Modern Anglicans do not sufficiently remember that the older Anglicanism was, in some important respects, a wider and worthier version of Christianity than that which for the last two centuries and more has monopolised the name.

In studying the history of the seventeenth century we have to remember that the mediæval tradition still exercised a potent authority over men's minds. In spite of all the rapid and considerable changes of religious opinion, which had successively secured the patronage of the State, the notion of orthodoxy as morally right and politically safe still governed the minds of statesmen. There was in this respect no substantial difference between Papist and Protestant, Arminian and Calvinist. Under James I. heretics were sent to the stake as under Henry VIII. or Henry IV., and, if it must be admitted that the executions under the former monarch had an anachronistic and extraordinary character, which certainly was absent in earlier times, yet the anachronism was rather felt than understood. The theory of religious persecution remained for the most part unsuspected and unchallenged. Protestants drew the line between permissible belief and unpardonable error at one point, Papists at another, but at some point both agreed that error was unpardonable, and therefore both illumined Smithfield with the fires of persecution. In England the course of events had secularised the persecuting authority. The Church had become irrecoverably discredited. It was impossible for men to retain any genuine respect for the ecclesiastical system, when they saw that it had become the patient victim of secular policy, and that it varied its form according to the requirements of the State. The spiritual prestige of the Papacy could not survive the Revolution, which had at once disproved its assumptions and disallowed its claims. To both the ecclesiastical system of the country and the Papacy the monarchy succeeded. Here, obviously, was a power capable of enforcing its own opinions. Here was an authority older than the Papacy, not less sanctioned by the Divine authority of Scripture, and not intrinsically less reasonable. Therefore, in England the monarch had taken a character which had no parallel in Christendom. Sir Thomas Overbury, in his *Observations on the State of France under Henry IV.*,[1] published in 1609, compares the state of the clergy in France and in England. In the former country, he says, the churchmen suffer more than either in England, where they wholly depend upon the King, or in Spain and Italy, where they wholly subsist by the Pope. This conception of the English Church as uniquely dependent upon the crown comes into prominence in many directions. When Dr. Mocket, the Warden of All Souls' College, published an apology of the Church of England, in which he seemed to suggest some independent right in the hierarchy, it was objected against him that he was guilty of presumption for undertaking such a task without commission from the King, "it being," says Fuller,[2] "almost as fatal for private persons

---

[1] Printed in Mr. Firth's *Stuart Tracts*, v. p. 223.
[2] *v. Church History of Britain*, vol. iii. p. 266. [London, 1837.]

to tamper with such public matters as for a subject to match into the blood royal without leave of his Sovereign." James I. regarded himself, and was regarded as, in the literal sense, a theological authority. He declared that of all his royal titles he valued most that of Defender of the Faith, which ascribed to him a spiritual function, which he was never slow to exercise. To this point we shall recur later. Here it is sufficient to indicate the necessarily monarchical aspect of the English Church. So long as that aspect commended itself as right to the conscience of ordinary Englishmen, the Church gained rather than lost in popular esteem by its dependence on the monarchy; and there were, in point of fact, reasons why this should for a long time be the case. When those reasons failed, and no fresh ones emerged, there was a great and ominous change in the popular sentiment.

As an excellent example of the state of the average Englishman's mind at the end of Elizabeth's reign, we cannot, perhaps, do better than accept a curious, and, in its way, excellent little book of devotion, published in the year 1591, and republished five years later. Its author was a layman named John Norden, who is known to have written a good many religious pamphlets during the reign of

James I. The book[1] is called *A Progress of Piety, whose Jesses lead into the Harbour of heavenly Heart's-ease, to recreate the afflicted souls of all such as are shut up in any inward or outward affliction.* Only three years had passed since the defeat of the great Armada, and the effect of that episode of national enthusiasm and triumph is apparent in the author's fervid loyalty, his intense belief in the Divine election and preservation of England, his fear and hatred, as much religious as patriotic, of Spain and the Papacy, his dread and dislike of sectaries and the endless disputes which they stirred up, his vein of puritan resentment at the growing disorder and luxury of social life. The paragraph entitled "A Motion to a Prayer for Queen Elizabeth, who as the Servant of the great King protecteth this Progress," expresses the conviction of ordinary religiously minded Englishmen at that time.

"What have we to do," he asks, "and what have we to think of our gracious Queen, chosen of the Lord himself, and miraculously preserved, and lovingly given us for our most especial good: by whom we have the freedom and liberty of the

---

[1] The book itself is very rare, only two copies, of which one is mutilated, being known to exist, according to the Parker Society's editor. I quote from the Parker Society's reprint, published in 1847.

Gospel, which is the path to our heavenly heart's ease: which before her days we know was stopt up with the briars and thorns of persecution and death, and now laid open again, as a most evident token that the Lord, by her sacred government, will lead his people through the wilderness of all the divisions, hurlyburlies, and tumults in this world; and to that end hath raised up many zealous, grave, and religious counsellors and godly ministers, who do direct the whole progress and marching on of her obedient people in the path of a godly profession of the word of God . . . ?"[1]

He urges the special reasons which the English have for carrying out the Pauline precepts of good citizenship. "If," he says, "we look into the present estate of our neighbours in foreign parts, it will, if we be not careless, strike us with terror, lest that God for our sins should also turn our peace into war, our plenty into want, and our comfort in her to misery and trouble by foreign enemies."[2] Then follows a long, eloquent, and fervid prayer for the Queen, which, in turn, is followed by "A Praise for her Majesty's most gracious government." The religious aspect of the monarchy excludes every other. Elizabeth is the commissioned and inspired servant of God.

---

[1] *v.* p. 38.   [2] *v.* p. 40.

"None ruleth here but she;
 Her heavenly guide doth shew,
How all things should decreed be
 To comfort high and low.

"Oh, sing then, high and low!
 Give praise unto the King
That made her queen; none but a foe
 But will her praises sing."[1]

This intense loyalty was connected necessarily with an equally intense dread and loathing of those allied powers of Spain and the Papacy in which Englishmen, then, saw the natural and ever-active foes of their religion and liberty. The memory of St. Bartholomew's Massacre (1572) was yet recent; the Spanish Armada (1588) had been a papal crusade; the Jesuits were in the meridian of their disastrous influence, and, as all the world believed, perhaps unfairly, but, surely, not without excuse, that influence was visible in the assassination or attempted assassination of the opponents of their policy. In 1584 Balthazar Gerard had murdered William of Orange, the heroic champion of Dutch independence; five years later Henry III. of France had fallen before the dagger of the priest Jacques Clement; plots against the life of Elizabeth were continually being discovered and announced by the government. The ordinary Englishman had some-

---

[1] *v.* p. 44.

thing more behind his horror of Rome than mere ignorance and prejudice. To his mind the conflict against the Spanish and papal alliance was something more than a chapter of normal politics. It was, he felt, a phase, the crucial phase, of that high mystic warfare in which God Himself and the Prince of Darkness are protagonists. The course of events seemed to confirm this view.

"England," says our author, "since it hath come to the taste of true religion, hath tasted how true it is that is said, that they that will live uprightly shall have many that will rise up against them. How hath the rage of Satan appeared against us, with bitter threats from Spain, with excommunications and condemnations from Rome! How have we been laboured to have been seduced by priests and seminaries from our bounden love and duty, not only towards her majesty, but towards our God. . . . How have they sought the death and destruction of our gracious queen and grave counsellors, by enchantments, by magic, by murder, by all devilish practices! Have we not been environed by fleets of foes at sea, by armies of rebels by land, and endangered by hidden traitors at home? Hath there yet any of their conspiracies prevailed? Hath not God stood our defence?"[1]

The same intense patriotism merging in, and in

---

[1] *v.* pp. 92, 93.

some sense fashioning, religious conviction determined the ordinary Englishman's mind with respect to the sectaries of his own country. They were "troublers of Israel": they weakened the Lord's host in the day of battle: they were sacrilegious rebels against the Lord's anointed.

"It is time for the children of God to take warning and be watchful, considering these dangerous times, wherein swarms of false prophets do everywhere fly to and fro to disquiet the godly, as Papists, Brownists, Anabaptists, the family of lust and lewdness, termed the Family of love; and many other dangerous sects, who seek to quench the ardent zeal of sincere Christianity, striving about words, which is to no profit, but to the perverting of the hearers."[1]

The two great controversies of the time are briefly considered, the one dealing with the ecclesiastical authority of the State, the other with the form of ecclesiastical government. "Whether they should obey the magistrate in ecclesiastical causes? and, Whether there should be a superiority or equality in church governors?" The author's conclusion is that of a man who personally dislikes controversy, but is conscious that there is some cause for it. His references to the clergy are curiously lacking in enthusiasm.

---

[1] *v.* p. 114.

"And for us that are the common people, that must expect to be fed by the ministry, let us pray for their unity, and that God will give them humble spirits, vigilant and watchful eyes, knowledge, love, zeal, and constancy, that the false prophets may be abandoned, and the true ministers of God be esteemed and embraced as the ministers of God."[1] The author holds a middle course. He deprecates the virulence of the contemporary critics of the hierarchy, but he holds that the hierarchy is not blameless. Indeed, the puritan sentiment which was destined to take such extreme expressions, when once it had become divorced from the national institutions of Church and State, is everywhere latent. The author exposes and denounces the current vices of society with prophetic fervour. It is evident enough that his loyalty to the established government is conditioned by its character as a protection against foreign tyranny and domestic corruption. Let that character be compromised or lost, and he will become the most dangerous of rebels. When James I. was negotiating with Spain, and when his hapless son committed himself to an ecclesiastical policy, which seemed to the mass of his subjects to be Roman in tendency, the belief in the Divine right of the monarchy as the foe of the Spanish power, secular and spiritual, inevitably died

---

[1] *v.* p. 118.

out, and was replaced by a sense of disappointment, almost of betrayal, in the minds of ordinary Englishmen. All the evidence we have proves that a rising wave of dissoluteness was passing over the country; partly, the sudden prosperity which followed the defeat of Spain and brought into the land great wealth and a reckless spirit of adventure, partly, the decay of all forms of moral discipline which resulted from the violent and frequent religious changes, may explain the fact; about the fact itself there can be no doubt. The deeper religious feeling of the country tended to take a puritan colour, and to inspire a severe theory of practical duty. It was the supreme misfortune of the National Church that, so far from drawing into itself this moral enthusiasm, it offended and drove it into revolt. No doubt Laud had his own notion of reforming society by the restoration of ecclesiastical discipline; but in that age, hardly less than in our own, that method of enforcing morality had an unreal and anachronistic aspect, and nowhere commanded either the confidence or the respect of the laity. Generally, the Court stood for moral licence, and the clergy stood for the Court. Puritan sentiment fastened on the strict observance of the Lord's Day, which was clothed with the attributes of the Jewish Sabbath; and both King and hierarchy authorised and encouraged the secularisation of the

Day. To be a sound Anglican at the end of Elizabeth's reign did still mean to be patriotic and puritan in sentiment though not in name: by the accession of Charles I. patriotism was suspicious of, and Puritanism hostile to, the National Church. A curious pamphlet in verse published in 1622 sufficiently indicates the change of sentiment. It is called "*The Interpreter, wherein three principal Terms of State, much mistaken by the vulgar, are clearly unfolded.*"[1] These terms are Puritan, Protestant, and Papist. The writer begins by asserting that these words no longer carry their old meanings.

> "Time was, a Puritan was counted such
> As held some ceremonies were too much
> Retained and urged; and would no Bishops grant,
> Others to rule, who government did want.
> Time was, a Protestant was only taken
> For such as had the Church of Rome forsaken;
> Or her known falsehoods in the highest point:
> But would not, for each toy, true peace disjoint.
> Time was, a Papist was a man who thought
> Rome could not err, but all her Canons ought
> To be canonical: and, blindly led,
> He from the Truth, for fear of Error, fled.
> But now these words, with divers others more,
> Have other senses than they had before:
> Which plainly I do labour to relate,
> As they are now accepted in our State."

Then follow the expositions of the terms as cur-

---

[1] *v. Stuart Tracts*, ed. Firth, pp. 233–244.

rently used. The Puritan is opposed to Spain, a hater of corruption in Church and State, regular and exact in his religious duties, an independent member of parliament, not to be frightened by courtiers out of his ancestral liberty.

> "His character abridged, if you would have,
> He's one, that would a Subject be, no Slave."

The term Protestant is next explained. He is all that the Puritan is not, a servile royalist, an opponent of the reformed cause on the continent, a supporter of every established abuse in Church and State, a time-server, an Erastian, and an unprincipled place-hunter.

> "A Protestant is such an other thing
> As makes, within his heart, God of the King.
>
> . . . . .
>
> A Protestant is he that with the stream
> Still swims, and wisely shuns every extreme;
> Loves not in point of faith to be precise;
> But to believe as Kings do, counts it wise:
>
> . . . . .
>
> A Protestant is an indifferent man,
> That with all faiths, or none, hold quarter can;
> So moderate and temperate his passion
> As he to all times can his conscience fashion.
>
> . . . . .
>
> His character abridged, if you will have,
> He's one that's no true Subject, but a Slave!"

The Papist's turn comes next. It needs no

saying that he is destitute of any redeeming virtue, but it is worth noticing that the anti-national aspect of Romanism is paramount. He is a tool of Spain and the slave of the Pope, ceaselessly at work against the interests of his own country. We have already pointed out the large plausibility of such a view at a time when every country in Europe was distracted with Jesuit intrigues.

The Church of England under James I. had, in truth, two very different aspects, and as the one or the other was seen, so was the Church admired or denounced. Unfortunately it was the worse rather than the better side which was most often in the view of Englishmen. Whatever the reasons, and some of them lie on the surface of history, the character of the Anglican clergy stood very low in the estimate of their own countrymen. Two authorities will suffice. In the year 1591 SPENSER published the remarkable satire on contemporary life called *Mother Hubbard's Tale*. There we find a description of the clergy which could hardly be surpassed in point of severity by the avowed enemies of the English Church. The Ape and the Fox, following their fortunes, fall in with a "formall Priest," with whom they enter into conversation, and whose advice they request as to their own best means of earning a maintenance. The Priest, rather flattered at the compliment, advises them to take Orders, and when the Ape objects that

> "The charge is wondrous great,
> To feed men's soules, and hath an heavie threat,"

he proceeds to reassure him by a candid description of clerical duty as currently understood.

> "Therefore herewith doo not your selfe dismay;
> Ne is the paines so great, but beare ye may,
> For not so great, as it was wont of yore;
> It's now a dayes, ne halfe so streight & sore.
> They whilom used duly everie day
> Their service & their holie things to say,
> At morne & even, besides their Anthemes sweete,
> Their penie Masses, and their Complynes meete,
> Their Diriges, their Trentals, & their shrifts,
> Their memories, their singings, & their gifts.
> Now all those needlesse works are laid away;
> Now once a weeke, upon the Sabbath day,
> It is enough to doo our small devotion,
> And then to follow any merrie motion.
> Ne are we tyde to fast, but when we list:
> Ne to wear garments base of wollen twist,
> But with the finest silkes us to array,
> That before God we may appear more gay.
>
> .   .   .   .   .
>
> We be not tyde to wilfull chastitie,
> But have the Gospell of free libertie."

Spenser incorporates into his satire the standing accusations against the clergy, which, from quite different standpoints, were persistently urged by Papists and Puritans: and there can be no reasonable doubt that those accusations contained a large element of truth. The abrupt termination of the old round of mechanical devotions, which had filled the time and occupied the energies of the parish clergy before the Reformation, had brought a strain upon the clerical character, which, speaking generally, it was unable to endure. Incumbents were not, for the most part, either saints or students. Without any very lofty devotional ideal to lift them, and with no living intellectual interest to stimulate their mental effort, they had, too often, nothing but their official system to hold them to duty, and that system then, as now, prescribed the veriest minimum of work, and left almost everything to the recognition and control of the parson's conscience.

A quarter of a century after Spenser published the satire from which I have quoted, that is, in the year 1615, RICHARD BAXTER was born. He has described in his *Autobiography* the ecclesiastical condition of the country in which he was reared. The description is a picture of the Jacobean Church of England drawn from life. "We lived," he says, "in a country that had but little preaching at all: in the village where I was born there was four Readers successively in six years time, ignorant men and two of them immoral in their lives; who were all my schoolmasters. In the village where my father lived, there was a Reader of about eighty years of age that never preached, and had two churches about twenty miles distant: his eyesight failing him, he said Common Prayer without book: but for the reading of the psalms and chapters, he got a common thresher and day-labourer one year, and a taylor another year: (for the clerk could not read well) and at last he had a kinsman of his own, (the excellentest stage-player in all the country, and a good gamester and a good fellow) that got Orders and supplied one of his places! After him another younger kinsman, that could write and read, got Orders: and at the same time another neighbour's son that had been awhile at school turn'd minister, and who would needs go further than the rest, ventur'd to preach (and after got a living in Staffordshire,) and when he had been a preacher about twelve or sixteen years, he was fain to give over, it being discovered that his Orders were forged by the first ingenious stage-player. After him another neighbour's son took Orders, when he had been awhile an attorney's clerk, and a common drunkard, and tipled himself into so great poverty that he had no other way to live: it was feared that he and more of them came by their Orders the same way with the forementioned person: These were the schoolmasters of my youth (except two of them:) who read Common Prayer on Sundays and holydays, and taught school and tipled on the weekdays, and

c

whipt the boys when they were drunk, so that we changed them very oft. Within a few miles about us were near a dozen more ministers that were near eighty years old apiece, and never preached: poor ignorant Readers, and most of them of scandalous lives: only three or four constant competent preachers lived near us, and those (though conformable all save one) were the common marks of the people's obloquy and reproach, and any that had but gone to hear them, when he had no preaching at home, was made the derision of the vulgar rabble, under the odious name of a Puritan."[1] Baxter goes on to describe the process by which he was led as a boy, almost in spite of himself, to associate the Church with moral laxity, and to connect serious religion with ecclesiastical censure. The account is so interesting in itself, and the point it illustrates is so important for the right understanding of that great revolt of the religious reason and conscience of the people which violently broke up the system of the National Church, and for ever destroyed the possibility of religious harmony in the country, that we may with advantage have it before us :—
" In the village where I lived the Reader read the

---

[1] *Reliquiae Baxterianae or, Mr. Richard Baxter's Narrative of the most memorable passages of his Life and Times, faithfully published from his own original manuscripts by Matthew Sylvester.* London, 1696, pp. 1, 2.

Common Prayer briefly, and the rest of the day even till dark night almost, except eating time, was spent in dancing under a may-pole and a great tree, not far from my father's door: where all the town did meet together: And though one of my father's own tenants was the piper, he could not restrain him, nor break the sport: so that we could not read the Scripture in our family without the great disturbance of the taber and pipe and noise in the street! Many times my mind was inclined to be among them, and sometimes I broke loose from conscience, and joyned with them; and the more I did it the more I was enclined to it. But when I heard them call my father *Puritan*, it did much to cure me and alienate me from them: for I consider'd that my father's exercise of reading the Scripture, was better than their's, and would surely be better thought on by all men at the last; and I considered what it was for that he and others were thus derided. When I heard them speak scornfully of *others* as Puritans whom I never knew, I was at first apt to believe all the lies and slanders wherewith they loaded them: But when I heard my own father so reproached, and perceived the drunkards were the forwardest in the reproach, I perceived that it was mere malice, For my father never scrupled Common-Prayer or ceremonies, nor spake against Bishops, nor ever so much as prayed but by a book or form, being not ever acquainted then with any that did otherwise: But only for reading Scripture when the rest were dancing on the Lord's Day, and for praying (by a form out of the end of the Common-Prayer Book) in his house, and for reproving drunkards and swearers, and for talking sometimes a few words of Scripture and the life to come, he was reviled commonly by the name of *Puritan*, *Precisian* and *Hypocrite*: and so were the godly conformable ministers that lived anywhere in the country near us, not only by our neighbours, but by the common talk of the vulgar rabble of all about us. By this experience I was fully convinc'd that godly people were the best, and those that despised them and lived in sin and pleasure, were a malignant unhappy sort of people: and this kept me out of their company, except now and then when the love of sports and play enticed me."[1]

Mr. Baxter senior represents at a later stage the same type of loyal religious Englishmen as John Norden, and we can see that the loyal ardour with which the latter accepted the system of Church and State is exchanged for a conscientious but reluctant acquiescence, which will not require much further provocation to become implacable resentment. He belonged to that large class of "conformable Puri-

[1] *Ibid.*, pp. 2, 3.

tans " who practised it (the Church system) out of policy, yet dissented from it in their judgments, who were, according to Fuller, the objects of Archbishop Harsnett's especial dislike. These men would normally be the backbone of the National Church, as they certainly were of the national morality; unhappily, to the Anglican hierarchy, preoccupied with its dream of rebuilding in England the imposing fabric of that ecclesiastical power, of which the name and framework yet survived in the country, they seemed nothing better than factious malcontents, to be discouraged and sternly held in check. So the breach grew steadily wider between the Church of England and the English conscience.

There was, as we have said, a worthier side to the Anglican Church. Three years after Spenser satirised the clergy in *Mother Hubbard's Tale* there issued from the press the first four books of RICHARD HOOKER's *Ecclesiastical Polity* (A.D. 1594), which not merely gave an intellectual justification for the Anglican system, but demonstrated its power to attract and hold the highest intelligence of the country. Hooker was but the most distinguished of a long series of apologists, who, with varying degrees of ability and learning, did battle with the enemy in the gate. As yet the line of defence was reasonable rather than traditional, an appeal to the intellect rather than to antiquity; and, so long as the domestic conflict with the Puritans was the principal issue, this character of Anglican apologetics was maintained; but as against the Roman attack, the patristic case for the Church of England was developed. The war was carried into the enemy's camp, and the appeal to Christian antiquity was successfully retorted on those who had too confidently pressed it. For such a controversy learning was indispensable, and the Anglican clergy were, and were regarded as, a learned clergy. England became the natural refuge of distressed scholars from abroad. The character of the King coincided with the temper of the Church. Mr. Mark Pattison's description of James's Court is worth quoting :—

"The reigning prince," he says, "was a lover, if not of learning, at least of a kind of theological lore which borrowed its lights from learning. James l. surrounded himself with divines whose talk was of fathers and councils. 'He doth wondrously covet learned discourse,' writes Lord Howard to Harrington, not indeed of the grand classical antiquity, for which none about him had eye or ear, but the bastard antiquity of the fourth century. They searched the ecclesiastical writers for precedents in support of English episcopacy, but they read them in the original, and this served to maintain Greek at a premium. For the first and the last time in our annals, the Court was the theatre of these learned discussions. Notwithstanding foibles which have handed down his character to ridicule, neither the understanding nor the attainments of James were contemptible. But his speech and action had a taint of puerility which degraded them. The ironical nickname of the British Solomon incurably clings to the only English prince who had carried to the throne knowledge derived from reading, or any considerable amount of literature. Despised by the men of business as a pedant, James had 'by far the best head in his council.' In the piteous condition of learning and the learned at that time, without patron or home, it was natural that the eyes of these outcasts of society should be directed to the only Court in Europe where their profession was in any degree appreciated."[1]

Casaubon, admittedly the foremost scholar of his time, found himself more and more out of sympathy with his Calvinist co-religionists. "The ministers of his own communion scouted antiquity of which they were ignorant, and which Casaubon regarded as the only arbiter of the quarrel. Books fell in his way written on this side of the Channel, in which he met with a line of argument very different from the uninstructed, but presumptuous dogmatism of the Calvinist ministers. He found to his surprise and delight that there were others

---
[1] *v. Isaac Casaubon*, p. 295.

besides himself who could respect the authority of the fathers, without surrendering their reason to the dicta of the papal Church. The young Anglo-Catholic school, which was then forming in England, took precisely the ground which Casaubon had been led to take against Du Perron."[1] Mr. Mark Pattison would explain the rise of what came to be the Laudian theory of the Church by the necessity, common to students as such, of finding in Christian antiquity an apology for the Reformation.

"Laud was the political leader, but in this capacity only the agent of a mode of thinking which he did not invent. Anglo-Catholic theology is not a system of which any individual thinker can claim the invention. It arose necessarily, or by natural development, out of the controversy with the papal advocates, as soon as that controversy was brought out of the domain of pure reason into that of learning. That this peculiar compromise, or *via media*, between Romanism and Calvinism developed itself in England, and nowhere else in Christendom, is owing to causes," which it did not lie within Mr. Mark Pattison's scheme to investigate, but which we may perhaps indicate. In England alone, thanks to the course of the Reformation, to the predominantly political character of the whole movement, to the theological idiosyncrasies of the English

---

[1] *Ibid.*, p. 299.

sovereigns, and, not least, to the deep, natural conservatism of the English mind, the Church had emerged from the religious revolution with much of its ancient aspect, much of its property, much of its constitutional importance. Therefore in England alone did the materials exist for a restoration of the ancient claims and forms of worship. The suggestions of Christian antiquity found natural embodiment in the actual system of the Church; the surviving mediæval framework seemed to require for its justification some renewal of the mediæval spirit. In Scotland, Germany, France, and Holland the destruction had been so complete that whatever existed had to find its origin and apology in the age itself, but in England so much of the old remained that a complete restoration was never apparently impossible.

Casaubon's arrival in England in 1610 is an event of considerable interest. It was not merely a striking proof of the intellectual prestige of the Jacobean Church, but also indicates the friendly attitude which was then maintained by Anglicans towards the non-episcopal Churches of the Continent. Archbishop Bancroft (whose famous sermon on Episcopacy in 1589 is considered to mark the definite beginning within the English Church of that insistence on the episcopal government, as alone divinely commissioned, which has in later times so far prevailed as to isolate the Church from all fellowship with the other reformed Churches) himself wrote to urge Casaubon's coming, and to promise him a prebendal stall at Canterbury. King James bestowed on him a pension of £300 a year from his own purse, and in the patent declared "his concurrancye with us and the Church of England in profession of religion." Archbishop Abbot, the puritanical successor of Bancroft, stood godfather to his English-born son, James. He became the personal friend of the leading English bishops. Casaubon, on his part, was delighted. "If I am not mistaken," he wrote, "the soundest part of the whole Reformation is to be found here in England, where the study of antiquity flourishes together with zeal for the truth." With Andrewes, then Bishop of Ely, he formed a close intimacy, and when he was dying that admirable prelate ministered to him the sacrament of Holy Communion; yet Casaubon had remained a member of the French congregation, and he had certainly neither received the rite of episcopal confirmation, nor episcopal ordination, nor had subscribed the Anglican formularies. There was nothing extraordinary in all this, and it did not attract any special notice. "Before the rise of the Laudian school, the English Church and the reformed Churches of the Continent mutually recognised each other as sisters." The supreme issue then was that conflict with the Papacy, which literally was a conflict for life and liberty. Not the most orthodox Anglican had any doubt as to his religious category. He stood with the rest of Protestants against the arch-enemy of Rome. How absorbing was that controversy is apparent from the pretentious but abortive scheme for founding a college in which the equipment of anti-papal controversialists should be systematically carried on. "It was intended," says Fuller, "for a spiritual garrison, with a magazine of all books for that purpose, where learned divines should study and write in maintenance of all controversies against the Papists. Indeed, the Romanists herein may rise up and condemn those of the Protestant confession. For as Solomon used not his military men for any servile work, in building the Temple, whereof the text assigneth this reason, 'For they were men of war,' so the Romish Church doth not burden their professors with preaching, or any parochial incumbrances, but reserves them only for polemical studies. Whereas in England the same man reads, preacheth, catechizeth, disputes, delivers sacraments, etc. So that, were it not for God's marvellous blessings on our studies, and the infinite odds of truth on our sides, it were impossible, in human probability, that we should hold up the bucklers against them. Beside the study of divinity, at the least two able historians were to be maintained in this College, faithfully and learnedly to record and publish to posterity all memorable passages in Church and Commonwealth."

"King James's College in Chelsea" was founded in 1610, and inaugurated with considerable éclat by the King himself; but it was doomed to a brief and stormy career, and scarcely outlived its first provost and real founder, the eccentric and munificent Sutcliffe.

Perhaps the most striking indication of the closeness of the ties which the common dread of Rome created between the Church of England and the other Protestant Churches is the fact that Anglican divines took their places with the members from the United States at the national synod at Dort, summoned in 1618 with the scarcely concealed intention of crushing the Arminians. The King took the keenest interest in the synod. He sent for the English deputies before their departure and gave them a list of instructions. They were to "inure themselves to the practice of the Latin tongue, that when occasion offered, they might deliver their minds with more readiness and facility"; they were always to act together, and in every possible way to promote ecclesiastical peace. On their arrival at Dort the English divines, on their admission to the synod, took an oath not to make use of any human writing, but only of God's Word for the certain and undoubted rule of faith. The States received them with much honour, and paid them an allowance of no less than £10 sterling a day, which they spent in 'keeping a table general,' where any fashionable foreigner was courteously and plentifully entertained.

Every week they sent an account of the proceedings to the King. When the Belgic Confession was offered for the acceptance of the members, Carleton, Bishop of Llandaff, in the name of the English deputies, approved all the points of doctrine, but made a protest on the subject of discipline, affirming "that the parity of ministers never prevailed in the Church." When, in April, 1619, the synod ended, the States presented every English deputy with a golden medal, and added £200 for the expenses of their return journey. The synod of Dort was, at the time, a notable triumph of Calvinism, but already there were signs that the Calvinistic theology was losing its hold upon the higher intelligence of the age. In England the rising school of Anglo-Catholics combined Arminian doctrines with their high ecclesiastical theory. Their extreme monarchical principles rendered them at once highly unpopular, and pleasing to the King. When James I. died in 1625, Calvinism was still the prevailing belief of religious Englishmen, but there was an anti-Calvinist movement among the clergy which had advanced with extraordinary quickness, and would drive a wedge between the mass of the laity and the more important clergy. It was a movement which appealed with success to the scholarly, devotional, and æsthetic instincts of English churchmen. It made rapid way in the universities. It was well represented in literature, especially in controversy. It was well organised, ambitious, and aggressive. In William Laud it found a whole-hearted exponent and an unflinching leader. In Charles I. it obtained a disciple and a patron. The royal prerogative was frankly placed at the service of a religious faction. For the first time since the Reformation the monarch openly played the rôle of an ecclesiastical partisan, and the party which the King favoured, however rich in personal distinction, however strong its intellectual position and equipment, was not that which, to the view of ordinary Englishmen, seemed most morally impressive. The association with the Court, which was licentious under James, and seemed to be papistical under Charles, went far to discredit the Arminian clergy. Inevitably that association drew in its train complicity with the unconstitutional and even tyrannous proceedings of the King. Laud's policy forced the fact on the notice of the country. He himself was practically chief minister of the Crown, and by a stroke of statecraft, on which he greatly plumed himself, the great office of Lord Treasurer was held by another bishop. In short, the clergy were tied hand and foot to the Crown precisely at the moment when the Crown was getting out of touch with the national sentiment. There was no reason in the nature of things why the constitutional revolution should have involved the total destruction of the ecclesiastical system, but, in the actual circumstances of the case, nothing else was possible. The hierarchy had been fashioned to the uses of the monarch, and had served his turn: for a few years his support had sustained it against the popular will, but when the day of reckoning came, and the monarch's power was broken before the accumulated difficulties of a political situation too artificial to be tolerable any longer, the hierarchy was helpless, and fell without a struggle. The great distinction between the præ-Laudian Church and the Church of later times lies here. The one, with all its faults, scandals, confusions, was genuinely national, and its dependence on the monarchy, however theoretically indefensible, did but express and make effective the fact. The other, with all its superiority of formal system, theory, and even practice, was always an artificial thing, and its constitutional dependence on the monarchy, developed and exaggerated under the coercion of its own religious theory, became ministerial to its unpopularity, weakness, and, finally, ruin. Precisely when the English people felt most keenly their fellowship with Protestant Europe in the desperate conflict with the mingled forces of the counter-Reformation, the Church of England began to adopt an attitude of exclusion towards the non-episcopalian Churches, and to elevate the matter of Church government into the category of religious essentials. The præ-Laudian Church was, in this respect also, a greater thing than its successor, and though the Calvinist theology and the conflict with Rome, which were the principal bases of unity, were not in themselves favourable to the highest spiritual results, yet, if only the intercommunion to which they led in the first instance had been maintained, it is impossible not to believe that both in England and on the Continent very happy consequences would have followed.

The præ-Laudian Church had the strength, the weakness, and the promise of a genuinely national character. It stood with the English people, sharing their prejudices, endorsing their ideals, consecrating their efforts, lifting their normal life; and, no doubt, it paid the price of this close alliance in a certain indifference to religious truth as such, an obvious lack of formal discipline, and an acquiescence in much that was limited and unworthy. But though there was thus weakness as well as strength in the position, there was certainly also an almost infinite hope ; for, so long as the Church remained the accepted exponent of the national faith and conscience, holding both (however inadequately) to the guidance and discipline of the Divine Gospel, it would follow that, as the national life developed, growing more complex, more refined, more weighted with responsibility, so—as from an inexhaustible treasury— would the Church draw from the national experience fresh illuminations of its message to humanity, fresh discoveries of duty, fresh fields of spiritual service. The brief triumph of Laudianism brought, as its first consequence, the violent overthrow of the constitution, political and ecclesiastical, and, as its abiding effect, the loss of the national character of the English Church. In the fervour of the political reaction which restored the monarchy and the hierarchy, and affirmed anew their inseparable connection, the old position seemed to have been recovered, and the Church of England again to have behind it the strength of the national confidence ; but, within a generation, the rift between the established system and puritan sentiment became more apparent than ever. The seventeenth century, which opens with the canons of 1603, which express the triumph of Anglicanism over the Puritans in the Hampton Court Conference, and which we may recognise as the rough draft of the Laudian scheme, ends with the Toleration Act of 1689, in which the defeat of that scheme was registered and declared, and the loss of national religious unity, which was the principal achievement of Laudianism, shown to be final. The Church of England remains to us now, national in name, in claim, and in sentiment, but not in fact. On the lines of the Laudian movement there was no real possibility of intellectual growth. English churchmen were invited to turn their backs on the present and to seek their precedents and ideals in a distant and ill-understood antiquity. Erudition, a somewhat archaic culture, art in so far as it was ecclesiastical, fine but rather artificial devotion, personal sanctity—all this was in the movement, and this is much ; but there was always this broad disadvantage that, on the Laudian principles, the Church of England fell apart from the main stream of national thought and feeling, becoming estranged from the deeper life of the people, and appearing in their eyes as an alien and artificial thing. Even so, I do not say that the balance of loss preponderates. To some minds, I know, there will be no question as to the religious gain ; but it is the loss which, perhaps, we most clearly perceive when we pass from the rough vigour of the præ-Laudian epoch to the unreal and petty conflicts of our own time.

Sabbatarianism

IN the Middle Ages no man needed to ask a reason for his obedience to the numerous and varied regulations imposed by the established system of religion. It was enough that the Church commanded, for the Church was, by universal agreement, divinely authorised to govern her children, and to dispute her right was obvious heresy to be abhorred of all faithful Christians. The Reformation for ever destroyed this unanimity of sentiment. The Church ceased to be above discussion, and became at a stroke the most freely discussed of all the institutions of society. Ecclesiastical authority was no longer the postulate of practical ethics. Men demanded a reason for every positive law which they obeyed. Why should they go to confession, hear mass, do penance, observe fast and festival, pay tithes, or indeed continue subject to any part of that great and complicated organisation of life by ecclesiastical rule, which had been the undisputed assumption of thought and life, but was now little more than a discredited and fading tradition? As a matter of fact, a clean sweep was made at the Reformation of most of the customary acts and disciplines of religion. Popular life was secularised, rationalised, and vulgarised by the process, which yet contained the promise of a higher spirituality and a more manly virtue than any which had before been attained. It was only by stages that the full content of the revolutionary process disclosed itself. First one and then another of the medieval arrangements was challenged, put on its trial, debated, and either rejected with contempt or furnished with a new title to acceptance. The creed, the government, the worship, the discipline, the customs of the Church, all in turn were subjected to this process, and the results varied according to a hundred circumstances of history, politics, and nationality. Of all Christian observances the dedication to religious uses of the first day of the week was the most venerable, popular, and important, and it did not occur to the first generation of reformers to question its claim on Christian regard, or to consider the nature and limits of the sanctity with which it was invested. Circumstances in England forced these issues into prominence, and led to results which have given a distinctive colour and direction to English Christianity.

Sabbatarianism is an insular development of the Reformation, and, alike in its origin and in its history, reflects the idiosyncrasy of the insular race. Had the presbyterian polity succeeded in establishing itself in England as well as in Scotland —and this at one time seemed likely enough—the rigours of the proverbial Scotch sabbath would have obtained over the whole island, but the triumph, after a stormy interval, of episcopalianism happily averted this disaster, and the triumph of sabbatarianism is no more than a curious and instructive episode in our ecclesiastical annals.

In the year 1583 a tragic accident at a bear-baiting in London, on Sunday afternoon, shocked the public conscience, and, being vigorously improved by the preachers, became the starting-point of a more careful observance of the Lord's Day than had generally prevailed. There had, as yet, been no sabbatarianism in the conduct of the Reformation, either at home or abroad. The royal injunctions of Edward VI. (1547) and Elizabeth (1559) had ordered the due religious observance of the day, but had not held that inconsistent with requiring the clergy to teach the people "that they may with a safe and quiet conscience, after their common prayer in the time of harvest, labour upon the holy and festival days, and save that thing which God hath sent"; and had even declared that not to do so on religious grounds would be grievously offensive and displeasing to God. The practice of the reformers, English and foreign, had been consistent with this view of Sunday observance. AYLMER, Bishop of London from 1567 to 1594, gave great offence to the Puritans by playing at bowls on Sunday, but he was only following the example of the great master, whom the Puritans exalted to an almost apostolic position, Calvin himself. "Indeed," observes Strype, commenting on the bishop's practice, "it was the general custom, both at Geneva and in all other places where Protestants inhabited, after the service of the Lord's Day was over, to refresh themselves with bowling, walking abroad, or other innocent recreations, and the bishop followed that which, in his travels abroad, he had seen ordinarily practised among them." Puritan sentiment was growing stronger among the religious laity at the end of Elizabeth's reign, and it naturally tended to attach itself to the one act of public religious observance which had survived the destructive process of reformation. The attitude of a prelate, who, beyond most of his brethren, had laid heavy hand on nonconforming parsons as naturally predisposed puritanically minded persons to accept the loftiest version of sabbatic obligation. In the year that followed Bishop Aylmer's death, *i.e.* 1595, a book appeared which is generally accepted as the first occasion of the protracted sabbatarian controversies of the seventeenth century. The author was a clergyman named NICHOLAS BOUND (or Bownde), at the time rector of Norton, in Suffolk, and his book was styled *The Doctrine of the Sabbath, plainly laid forth, and soundly proved by testimonies both of Holy Scripture, and also of old and new ecclesiastical writers*. It was dedicated to no less a personage than Robert Devereux, Earl of Essex, at the moment a popular favourite and well regarded at Court. Fuller[1] has set down under eleven heads the main propositions of this book, and as they formed the texts of heated controversy, we may usefully reproduce some of them here. Dr. Bound maintained:—

1. That the commandment of sanctifying every seventh day, as in the Mosaical Decalogue, is moral and perpetual.
2. That whereas all other things in the Jewish Church were taken away (priesthood, sacrifices, and sacraments), this Sabbath was so changed that it still remaineth.
3. That there is great reason why we Christians should take ourselves as straitly bound to rest upon the Lord's Day, as the Jews were

---

[1] *v. Church History*, book ix. chaps. 20, 21 (vol. iii. p. 143. London, 1837).

upon their Sabbath, it being one of the moral commandments, where all are of equal authority.

4. The rest upon this day must be a notable and singular rest, a most careful, exact, and precise rest, after another manner than men are accustomed.

The remaining propositions apply the principles here stated to the main classes of human action. The author falls away from the sustained severity of his teaching when he exempts "lords, knights, and gentlemen of quality" from his prohibition of solemn feasts and wedding-dinners on the Lord's Day; but with this exception he is a thorough-going sabbatarian. The effect produced by this volume was immediate and considerable. "It is almost incredible how taking this doctrine was," remarks Fuller, "partly because of its own purity and partly for the eminent piety of such persons as maintained it, so that the Lord's Day, especially in corporations, began to be precisely kept, people becoming a law to themselves, forbearing such sports as yet by statute permitted; yea, many rejoicing at their own restraint herein." Among educated and religious persons there was by no means general acceptance of Dr. Bound's opinions. Fuller's account cannot be improved upon, and it has the advantage of belonging to the age.

"Learned men," he says, "were much divided in their judgments about these sabbatarian doctrines. Some embraced them as ancient truths consonant to Scripture, long disused and neglected, now seasonably revived for the increase of piety. Others conceived them grounded on a wrong bottom; but, because they tended to the manifest advance of religion, it was pity to oppose them, seeing none have just reason to complain, being deceived into their own good. But a third sort flatly fell out with these positions, as galling men's necks with a Jewish yoke, against the liberty of Christians: that Christ as Lord of the Sabbath had removed the rigour thereof, and allowed men lawful recreations: that this doctrine put an unequal lustre on the Sunday on set purpose to eclipse all other holydays, to the derogation of the authority of the Church: that this strict observance was set up out of faction to be a character of difference, to brand all for libertines who did not entertain it."

Bound's book was not left unanswered long. Another Suffolk incumbent, THOMAS ROGERS, rector of Horningsheath, led the way in defending the traditional view, as he proudly affirms in the preface to a work on the Thirty-nine Articles, published in 1607. This preface, inscribed to Archbishop Bancroft, is a document of considerable interest and importance, and will reward anyone, desirous of knowing the accepted view of the English Church in the early seventeenth century, who will be at the pains to read it. After tracing rapidly the course of the Reformation in England, and exulting in the defeat of all enemies of the Church establishment both at home and abroad, he goes on to speak of the fresh outbreak of disaffection, which had taken the form of "Sabbath speculations and presbyterian (that is more than kingly or popely) directions for the observation of the Lord's Day."[1]

"In this their sally," he says, "they set not upon the bishops and their calling, their chancellors, etc., as popish and anti-christian: they let them alone, seeing and knowing they are too well backed for them to subvert: but (which are of great all, and almost of the same antiquity with bishops divers of them, and I had almost said as necessary) they ruinate, and at one blow beat down all times and days, by just authority destined to religious and holy uses, besides the Lord's Day, saying plainly and in peremptory words, that the Church hath none authority, ordinarily, or from year to year perpetually to sanctify any other day to those uses, but only the Lord's Day." He gives some specimens

---

[1] *v. The Catholic Doctrine of the Church of England:* an Exposition of the XXXIX. Articles, by Thomas Rogers, A.M., Chaplain to Archbishop Bancroft, p. 18. [Parker Society.]

of the new teaching which had come to his knowledge. "I have read (and many there be alive which will justify it) how it was preached in a market-town in Oxfordshire, that to do any servile work or business on the Lord's Day is as great a sin as to kill a man, or to commit adultery. It was preached in Somersetshire that to throw a bowl on the Sabbath day is as great a sin as to kill a man. It was preached in Norfolk, that to make a feast or wedding-dinner on the Lord's Day is as great a sin as for a father to take a knife and cut his child's throat. It was preached in Suffolk (I can name the man, and I was present when he was convented before his ordinary for preaching the same), that to ring more bells than one upon the Lord's Day to call the people unto the church is as great a sin as to commit murder."[1] These monstrous extravagances, scarcely explicable, and in no respect to be excused, by the enthusiasm of conviction and the delusive vehemence of rhetoric, naturally shocked Mr. Rogers deeply, and he lost no time in setting the authorities to work.

"It is a comfort unto my soul, and will be till my dying hour, that I have been the man and the means, that these sabbatarian errors and impieties are brought into light and knowledge of the State: whereby whatsoever else, sure I am, this good hath

---
[1] *Ibid.*, p. 19.

ensued, namely, that the said books of the Sabbath (comprehending the above-mentioned, and many more such fearful and heretical assertions) have been both called in, and forbidden any more to be printed and made common. Your Grace's predecessor, Archbishop Whitgift, by his letters and officers at synods and visitations, anno 1599, did the one: and Sir John Popham, Lord Chief Justice of England, at Bury St. Edmund's in Suffolk, anno 1600, did the other."[1] Rogers, in the course of his commentary on the Articles, succeeds in getting in a good many effective thrusts against his opponent, and he certainly makes good his opinion that the sabbatarian movement was directly connected with the anti-hierarchical crusade of the Puritans. In truth, their sabbatarian doctrine was double-edged, and with both edges it cut away the authority of the Church. On the one hand, it denied the right of the Church to institute holy days, and, by insisting on their observance, to impinge upon the divinely certified right of every man to labour six days in the week.[2] On the other hand, by insisting

---

[1] *Ibid.*, p. 20.

[2] *Ibid.*, p. 322. "It sheweth also the boldness of our home adversaries, the Puritan Dominicans, which say, that the Church nor no man can take away the liberty (of working six days in the week) from men, and drive them to a necessary rest of the body upon any day saving the seventh."

cf. The London Petition against Episcopacy in 1640. The

on the divine institution of the Christian Sabbath, it implicitly repudiated the ecclesiastical claim to the appointment and regulation of the Lord's Day. Moreover, as it inevitably linked itself to the puritan exaltation of "the Ministry of the Word" in preaching as the Christian analogue of the prophetic witness under the Jewish system, it lent itself to collision with the established Church system on another side, on that side on which the Church system was notoriously weak. "We damn ourselves" —such is Rogers's summary of the sabbatarian view—"if we go not from those ministers and churches where the scriptures and homilies only be read, and seek not unto the prophets, when (and so often as) we have them not at home."[1] The arguments of Mr. Rogers, though backed by the efforts of the authorities as well ecclesiastical as civil, were powerless to arrest a movement which, in spite of

---

twenty-second head of grievances is this: "The pressing of the strict observation of the Saints' days, whereby great sums of money are drawn out of men's purses for working on them; a very high Burthen on most people, who getting their living on their daily Employments, must either omit them, and be idle; or part with their money, whereby many poor families are undone, or brought behindhand: yet many Churchwardens are sued, or threatened to be sued, by their troublesome Ministers, as perjured persons, for not presenting their Parishioners who failed in observing Holy days."—*v.* Rushworth, vol. iv. p. 95.

[1] *Ibid.*, p. 327.

its fanaticism and extravagance, did express the serious moral purpose of the nation at the time.

"The price of the doctor's book began to be doubled: as commonly books are then most called on when called in, and many who hear not of them when printed inquire after them when prohibited: and though the book's wings were clipped from flying abroad in print, it ran the faster from friend to friend in transcribed copies: and the Lord's Day in most places was most strictly observed. The more liberty people were offered, the less they used it, refusing to take the freedom authority tendered them."[1] A few years later the sabbatarian controversy leapt into the front rank of political questions. James I., with his wonted confidence and something less than his natural astuteness, thrust himself into the fray.

In 1618 James, then on his way back from Scotland, had been appealed to by divers Lancashire magnates for relief from the sabbatarian rigour of the local ministers and magistrates, who had begun to suppress the customary Sunday recreations. The King gave a hasty decision in favour of the complainants, and continued his journey. The consequences might have been expected. It was not in human nature not to abuse the victory, and abused it was. The Sunday amusements became

---

[1] Fuller, *loc. cit.*, p. 146.

more aggressive and less respectable than ever. Many of the Lancashire magnates were Roman Catholics, and had other reasons for rejoicing in the opportunity of humiliating their intolerant neighbours. The disturbance became more serious than before, and the King's interference again was invoked. Acting on the advice of the Bishop of Chester, at that time the excellent and conciliatory Morton, James issued a declaration, which limited the liberty of Sunday recreations to those of his subjects who attended the church service, thus chastening the unholy glee of the Papists. It is a characteristically Jacobean composition, too long to quote in full, but hardly to be compressed without injustice. The King scolds impartially both Papists and Puritans, and grants his indulgence on terms which secured the discontent of both. The crucial paragraph is the following :—

"Our pleasure is that the bishop of that diocese take the like strait order with all the Puritans and Precisians within the same, either constraining them to conform themselves or to leave the county, according to the laws of our kingdom and canons of our Church, and so to strike equally on both hands against the contemners of our authority and adversaries of our Church : and as for our good people's lawful recreation, our pleasure likewise is, that after the end of divine service our good people be not disturbed, letted, or discouraged from any lawful recreation, such as dancing, either men or women; archery for men, leaping, vaulting, or any other such harmless recreation, nor from having of May-games, Whitsun-ales, and Morris-dances; and the setting up of May-poles and other sports therewith used: so as the same be had in due and convenient time, without impediment, or neglect of divine service: and that women shall have leave to carry rushes to the church for the decorating of it, according to their old custom: but withal we do here account still as prohibited all unlawful games to be used on Sundays only, as bear and bull-baitings, interludes, and (at all times in the meaner sort of people by law prohibited), bowling."[1]

Hardly had the royal author of this curious homily arrived home, than he reissued it for the whole kingdom, requiring the bishops to order it to be read in all the parish churches. In adopting this method of publishing the proclamation, James, in Dr. Gardiner's words "hit upon a plan which was calculated to rouse the greatest possible amount of opposition."[2] So general and so vehement was

---

[1] The Declaration as reissued and slightly enlarged by Charles I. is printed in Gee and Hardy's *Documents illustrative of English Church History*, pp. 528-32. [London, 1896.]

[2] *History of England* (in ten vols.), vol. iii. p. 251. [London, 1895.]

the discontent, and even open resistance, that the King had the prudence to give way, and withdraw the order. Fifteen years later, in 1633, when the puritan movement had immensely gained strength from the fatuous proceedings of the government, Charles I. had the temerity to reissue his father's unfortunate declaration. In the interval a change of no slight importance had happened at Lambeth. Archbishop Abbot had died in 1632, and been succeeded by Archbishop Laud, and the adoption of a vigorous policy against Puritanism was the immediate consequence of the change. When, some years later, the Puritans had their old enemy in their power, the accusation was pressed against him that he had been responsible for reviving and enlarging this declaration. It was said that he "laboured to put a badge of holiness, by his breath, upon places, and to take it away from days," and that he had designed to "take away preaching." The archbishop denied the accusation, no doubt sincerely; the act was the King's without question, but there was so much truth in the puritan case, that the primate's great influence with the King had certainly not been used in the interest of indulgence. Laud retorted on his adversaries with some effect the teaching of Calvin and the practice of Geneva. "The book names (he said) none but lawful recreations: therefore, if any unlawful be used, the book gives them no warrant. And that some are lawful, (after the public service of God is ended,) appears by the practice of Geneva, where, after evening prayer, the elder men bowl, and the younger train. And Calvin says in express terms, that one cause of the institution of the sabbath was, 'that servants might have a day of remission from their labour': and what time of the day fit, if not after evening prayer? and what rest is there for able young men, if they may use no recreation?' . . . 'I pray God keep us in the mean, in this business of the sabbath, as well as in other things, that we run not into a Jewish superstition, while we seek to shun profaneness. This Calvin hath in the meantime assured me, 'that those men who stand so strictly upon the morality of the sabbath, do by a gross and carnal sabbatization, three times outgo the superstition of the Jew.'"[1]

There is something oddly pathetic in the spectacle of Archbishop Laud warning those strong iconoclasts against superstition. That the warning was necessary cannot be questioned. The sabbatarianism of the Puritans had already passed into fanaticism as a doctrine, and into superstition as a practice; and yet it is certain that in their hands lay in that critical epoch the task of destroying

---

[1] *Laud's Works*, vol. iv. pp. 252-5. [Library of Anglo-Catholic Theology.]

superstition in Church and State, and the archbishop, in spite of the justice of his argument on the specific issue, in spite of the apparent reasonableness of his mental attitude towards the practical question, was truly standing for superstition in Church and State. Perhaps the key to the paradox lies here. The Puritan deferred to an authority, which, however, for a time, he might disguise from himself and from others its true character, was, in the last analysis, the authority of his own reason and conscience. His high-sounding appeals to the divine law, written in the primal nature of man, reaffirmed with awful solemnity amid the thunder of Sinai, bound anew with fresh and more moving sanctions on the Christian, were really, though he did not suspect it, so many appeals to himself. In his moral repugnance against the aggressive profligacy of a society, which was, for quite intelligible reasons, unusually profligate, in his righteous resentment against a *soi-disant* spiritual government, which seemed habitually to depress religious enthusiasm, and to spread its shield over lax morals and apparent irreligion, the Puritan became fanatical, and in his fanaticism degenerated quickly into absurdity and intolerance; but he was under no permanent disqualifications in the matter of education by experience. He could unlearn his own errors and undo his own mistakes, for the authority which determined his course was that of his own understanding, and that grew wiser and more trustworthy under the disciplines of life. But the Anglicanism of Laud was intrinsically unteachable, and therefore ultimately, morally and mentally, enfeebling also. No doubt at the moment its very principles of dependence on Catholic precedents and the royal prerogative secured it against the practical extravagances which disgraced and discredited the Puritans; for the appeal to Christian antiquity was in some sense an appeal to human experience, and the royal prerogative was a political authority in direct contact with the actual life of the nation; and, accordingly, both prohibited such grotesquely impracticable conceptions of Christian duty as were solemnly proclaimed and defended by men who ignored everything but the text of scripture. The disadvantage of governing conduct by reference to an external authority—discoverable in the past, actually, though not theoretically, irreformable in the present, and expressed in a series of rigid precedents—would become manifest as society developed new wants and passed under new conditions. And the defects of the royal prerogative as an instrument for regulating the religious practice of the nation would become apparent precisely in proportion to the strength and purpose of the national religious sentiment. It is true that considerations of reason and expediency were frequently advanced in support of ecclesiastical rules, but we feel as we read the Laudian arguments that these are not the really determining elements in the reasoning.

On the sabbatarian question, which directly touched the procedure of common life at so many points, Laudianism is seen at its best and Puritanism at its worst; and yet, as far as I can appreciate the facts, the best intelligence (outside the universities, where anti-puritan views prevailed) and the deepest piety of the country were rather puritan than Laudian, until the excesses of the more violent and fanatical sabbatarians who came to power for a few years during the Commonwealth, created the revulsion of feeling which found expression in an outbreak of profanity of all kinds under Charles II. This revulsion was itself but a temporary aberration. There was a return to something like puritan severity before the century closed, and the leading Anglican clergy of the Revolution period insisted strongly on the strict observance of the Lord's Day. James I.'s declaration in favour of Sunday recreations would have been hardly less unpalatable to the founders and patrons of the societies for the reformation of manners than to the victims of the High Commission. At the time men were mostly impressed by the incongruity of the alliance between the hierarchy and the laxer classes of society.

THOMAS MAY bore no high character with his own contemporaries, but he was a keen and well-informed observer of events, and there can be no reason to doubt the substantial truth of his description of the impression made on the public mind by the action of the church authorities with respect to the sabbatarian movement. " The like unhappy course did the clergy take to depress Puritanism, which was ' to set up irreligion itself against it,' the worst weapon which they could have chosen to beat it down ; which appeared especially in point of keeping the Lord's Day, when not only books were written to shake the morality of it, as that of *Sunday no Sabbath*,[1] but sports and pastimes of jollity and lightness were permitted to the country people upon that day, by public authority, and the warrant commanded to be read in churches : which, instead of producing the intended effect, may credibly be thought to have been one motive to a stricter observance of that day in that part of the kingdom which before had been well devoted ; and many men, who before had been loose and careless, began upon that occasion to enter into a more serious

---

[1] This book was written by John Pocklington, Rector of Yelden and Canon of Windsor. It was ordered to be publicly burned in 1640, and its author was deprived of his preferments. Dr. Bray, who had licensed his works, was enjoined to preach a recantation sermon in St. Margaret's, Westminster.

consideration of it, and were ashamed to be invited by the authority of churchmen to that which themselves at the best could but have pardoned in themselves as a thing of infirmity." He adds that "the example of the court, where plays were usually presented on Sundays, did not so much draw the country to imitation, as reflect with disadvantage upon the court itself, and sour those other court pastimes and jollities, which would have relished better without that in the eyes of all the people, as being things that had ever been allowed to the delights of great princes."[1]

No doubt, as we have said, there was a change of feeling when the controversy had come into the hands of the uneducated classes, and, under the terrible strain of the Civil War, these had broken out in astonishing exhibitions of fanaticism. There was a reaction against the presumptuous dogmatism, the tyrannous intolerance, the meddlesome inquisitions of zealots, whose personal character did not commend their authority.

Fuller, himself in feeling and habit a Puritan, writes with evident disgust of the general moral decline which showed itself among the more vehement sectaries, and, oddly enough, beginning with an

---

[1] *v. History of the Parliament of England*, by Thomas May, p. 24. [Oxford, 1854.]

exaggerated emphasis on the duty of observing the sabbath, ended by repudiating the positive law altogether. It was a logical development of sabbatarian contempt for church authority in one direction, as the rise of the Seventh Day Baptists was in another. "But here," he says, "it is much to be lamented, that such who, at the time of the sabbatarian controversy, were the strictest observers of the Lord's Day, are now ruled by their violence into another extreme—to be the greatest neglecters, yea, contemners thereof. These transcendents, accounting themselves mounted above the predicament of common piety, aver they need not keep any, because they keep all days Lord's Days, in their elevated holiness. But, alas! Christian duties, said to be ever done, will prove never done, if not *sometimes* solemnly done. These are the most dangerous levellers, equalling all times, places, and persons, making a general confusion to be gospel-perfection. Whereas, to speak plainly, we in England are, *rebus sic stantibus*, concerned now more strictly to observe the Lord's Day than ever before. Holy days are not, and holy eves are not, and Wednesday and Friday litanies are not, and Lord's Day eves are not; and now some out of error, and others out of profaneness, go about to take away the Lord's Day also. All these things make against God's solemn and public service."

Perhaps the most astonishing evidence of the confusion of the religious intelligence by the sabbatarian controversies is presented by the account of a discussion in Cromwell's parliament in 1657, which is given in BURTON's Parliamentary Diary.[1] A bill for securing the better observance of the Lord's Day was read and debated. There was much difference of opinion among the members as to the limits of legitimate Christian action on the sacred day. There was a severe party in the House which would make "unnecessary walking" a punishable offence, and even "idle sitting, openly, at gates or doors, or elsewhere," but there yet survived in the fanatical assembly some elements of good sense, and even some vestiges of humour, so that, on these points, a considerable and vehement debate was carried on. "I except against the words in the bill," said one member, "'idle sitting, openly, at gates or doors, or elsewhere'; and 'walking in churchyards, etc.' Let a man be in what posture he will, your penalty fines him." Another objected to the word "elsewhere," for "he knew not how far this may reach." Major-General Whalley raised the question of health. "God requires not these things of us," he

---

[1] *Diary of Thomas Burton, Esq.*, member in the Parliaments of Oliver and Richard Cromwell from 1656 to 1659, edited by John Towill Rutt, vol. ii. pp. 261–8. [London, 1828.]

said. "We must take heed of adding to the commandment of God. If you put this clause, you deprive men of the very livelihood they have by the air; as at Nottingham, many people that have houses in the rock, and have no air, live most part of their time without doors." This consideration was not without effect. One member sarcastically suggested that the proposed clause was inadequate, and urged that it should include "leaning or standing at doors." His levity was gravely rebuked by another member, who would, however, make a distinction between "working" and "sitting at doors." The law officers now intervened on the side of practical common sense. "In some parts of this city," said the Master of the Rolls, "unless people have liberty to sit at doors, you deprive them of most of the air they have all the week, and destroy their children." The Lord Chief Justice followed on the same side, pointing out that, if the clause were adopted, it would probably "cause discord and prying amongst neighbours into the actions of one another."

The rigid sabbatarians remained obdurate. "You had as good leave out the whole bill as leave out this clause," said Major Burton. "Follow out your principle logically," was the rejoinder, "and where will it carry you? Why stop at the doorstep? There may be profaneness by sitting under some eminent tree in a village, or an arbour, or Gray's Inn walks." In the division the clause was lost by the narrow majority of two votes. Encouraged with this success, the rational party now pressed for the withdrawal of the bill, and raised the formidable plea of conscientious doubt. Major-General Desborough had scruples as to the proper duration of Sunday. Did the sabbath day begin at twelve o'clock on Saturday night, or not? Colonel Holland was in the same perplexity, and made an interesting personal admission. "Divers godly precious people," he said, "are unsatisfied about the institution of the day. And as to time, it is likewise scrupled by many godly men, who think that only twelve hours is the sabbath day. It is rejoicing of the heart in observing a day to the Lord. It is better than one thousand days to be pinned up in a place. I was once when I would have gone to six or seven sermons on a day. I am not so now. I do not make so much conscience of it now, but do think that I may serve God as well at home with godly servants and other people. I am for the observation of a day as much as any man, and though there were no precept for it, every man by nature is tied to it. I would have it adjourned." The effect of this frank but indiscreet utterance was unfortunate. The time had not yet come when sermons could be so slightingly spoken about. The debate proceeded amid some uproar, and in the end the bill passed the House. Colonel Holland's speech, in the character of the emancipated Puritan, appears to reflect the teaching of the Quakers, which with respect to the observance of the Lord's Day, as to other matters of current controversy, commended itself amid the general distraction as obviously reasonable. At that early stage of the Quaker movement popular attention was mainly arrested by the extraordinary exhibitions of fanaticism on the part of individuals, such as the unhappy Nayler, whose case occupied the attention of the very parliament from whose proceedings we have made some extracts; but the real strength of George Fox's protest against the existing ecclesiastical systems of his time lay in its correspondence with the practical good sense of a community, wearied beyond endurance by the conflicts of sects. BARCLAY's *Apology* was not published until 1675, and in the interval the Quakers had to a great extent outgrown their earlier extravagances; but the fundamental reasonableness of his general attitude was present from the first in their teaching. I do not know a better summary of the reasonable case for Lord's Day observance than that of the Quaker apologist.

"We, not seeing any ground in scripture for it, cannot be so superstitious as to believe, that either the Jewish sabbath now continues, or that the first day of the week is the antitype thereof, or the true Christian sabbath; which with Calvin we believe to have a more spiritual sense; and therefore we know no moral obligation by the fourth command, or elsewhere, to keep the first day of the week more than any other, or any holiness inherent in it. But first, forasmuch as it is necessary that there be some time set apart for the saints to meet together to wait upon God; and that, secondly, it is fit at some times they be freed from their outward affairs; and that, thirdly, reason and equity doth allow that servants and beasts have some time allowed them to be eased from their continual labour; and that, fourthly, it appears that the apostles and primitive Christians did use the first day of the week for these purposes; we, finding ourselves sufficiently moved for these causes, to do so also, without superstitiously straining the Scriptures for another reason; which, that it is not to be there found, many Protestants, yea, Calvin himself, upon the fourth command hath abundantly evinced. And though we therefore meet, and abstain from working upon this day, yet doth not that hinder us from having meetings also for worship at other times."[1] The Quaker statement of the obligation to observe the Lord's Day builds everything on

---

[1] Barclay's *Apology*, tenth edition, p. 330. [London, 1841.]

reason and expediency, nothing on any authority whether of natural law, or of the decalogue, or of the Church, and therefore, almost alone among the doctrinal statements of the seventeenth century, it remains still vital and satisfying to that comparatively small class, to whom reason and expediency are sufficient governors of practice; but then, as ever since, the mass of men want some more apparent and impressive authority to hold them to their duty, and that authority was sought then, as now, in two directions, either in the Bible or in the Church. The mere stating of the alternative indicates the religious and political affinities which would reveal themselves in the sabbatarian controversy. Puritan sentiment, as we have said, inevitably predisposed men to take up that view of the question which minimised, or wholly ignored, the authority of the Church, and gave a divine sanction to civic disloyalty, when an anti-puritan monarch ordered anti-sabbatarian proceedings. Anglican sentiment, as inevitably, predisposed men to take up the opposite view, which magnified ecclesiastical authority, and seemed to disprove the puritan contempt for the Church by exhibiting the unconscious subjection to its law implied in the puritan practice, and added an element of religious zeal to their natural disposition to support an anti-sabbatarian monarch, who was also a sound Anglican.

Thus an unconscious hypocrisy pervades the whole conflict, the combatants are governed by other reasonings than they acknowledge or suspect; sacred names are written on the rival banners, but the determining influences throughout are more political than religious. Individuals, of course, were in deadly earnest, and when once the passion of fanaticism had been set ablaze in the nation, though the motives from which the conflagration sprang were properly political, yet the consequences were the genuine and normal products of fanaticism. On both sides arguments were pressed to their extremest conclusions, logic counted for more than it was worth in a discussion which touched the delicate and complicated procedure of human life; when the great deeps were stirred, controversy could no more be penned within the enclosures of knowledge and reason, but became the interest and the victim of ignorance and folly, until a cessation of the conflict came from the exhaustion of the combatants and the general disgust of the people. English good sense, as usual, steered the middle way. The puritan sabbath was not able to maintain itself in national acceptance, and no portion of the vast mass of dead literature which the seventeenth century has bequeathed to us is more incapable of resuscitation than the storehouse of perverted erudition and grotesque reasoning which the sabbatarian conflict created; yet it is not less certain that that conflict made an abiding impression on the national life. The tradition of Lord's Day observance which survived was neither Puritan nor Anglican, but a blending of both. Less austere than the one, more conscientious than the other, it commended itself to the deliberate approval of a people, averse to rigorous theories, curiously sensitive to practical obligations.

An excellent example of the more sober Puritan teaching on the subject of Lord's Day observance is afforded by a sermon of the famous Puritan scholar, DR. JOHN LIGHTFOOT (1602–1675), Master of Catherine Hall, Cambridge, whose works are still used by biblical students.[1] In spite of his Puritanism, in spite of the fact that he had received preferment from the rebel government and had even pronounced a panegyric on the Protector, he was exempted from the eviction which seemed to await him at the Restoration, because the fame of his learning commanded the admiration even of the royalists. To his own honour Sheldon, Archbishop of Canterbury, stood his friend, and confirmed him in his preferments. These particulars will make it evident that the sabbatarian views of Lightfoot cannot be discounted on the grounds of his ignor-

---

[1] The sermon is printed in vol. vii. pp. 367–90 of Lightfoot's Works, edited by Pitman. [London, 1822.]

ance, or fanaticism, or unimportance. The text of the sermon in question is the fourth commandment, and, after some general observations on the creation, the preacher attacks his subject. Of course, the narrative in Genesis is accepted as in the strictest sense record of fact, and much that is not in the narrative is read into it. What could be more suggestive of the chasm which parts the educated thought of our own day from that of the age, which fixed the subscriptions and formularies of the modern Anglican Church, than this?

"That the world was made at equinox all grant, but differ at which, whether about the eleventh of March or twelfth of September; to me in September without all doubt. All things were created in their ripeness and maturity: apples ripe and ready to eat, as is too sadly plain in Adam and Eve's eating the forbidden fruit."

Lightfoot then *proves* that Adam fell on the very day that he was created, "about the sixth hour, or high noon most probably, as that was the time of eating." That on the same afternoon Christ was promised, and on the following day God ordained, and Adam kept, the Sabbath. Thus the Gospel preceded the institution of the Sabbath, and the obligation to keep it holy rests both on the law of nature written in man's heart and on "evangelical revelation." The observance of the Sabbath was binding on Adam's posterity, because the Sabbath corresponds to the nature of man. All varieties of law—moral, commemorative, evangelical, typical—combine in the law of the Sabbath. The patriarch of the race set an example for perpetual imitation. He kept the Sabbath, most probably by sacrificing the animals whose skins were subsequently appointed for his clothing. Here follows a description of Adam's preaching to his family circle upon the Sabbath Day, which may interest students of *Paradise Lost* as providing a curious parallel to Milton's description of the theological disquisitions which relieved the tædium of paradise. The first man, of course, displays the developed orthodoxy of the seventeenth century. Having thus rooted his case for the Sabbath in the very circumstances of the creation, the preacher conceives himself to have avoided the current controversies.

"The consideration of these ends of the Sabbath may serve to assoil that controversy about the antiquity of its institution, viz. whether its institution was not before the giving of the law? In the dispute about the Sabbath, a-foot in England some years ago, there were some went so high (shall I say?) or so low, as to maintain that our Sabbath was not of Divine institution, but ecclesiastical only; not ordained by God, but the Church. And to make good this assertion they would persuade you that there was no Sabbath instituted before the giving of the law." This view, of course, is summarily dismissed as not only inconsistent with the evidence of Scripture, but also as obscuring the "beauty of the Sabbath" as ancient, universal, divinely exemplified, and intrinsically noble. "It reacheth, as the cherubims' wings, from one end of the world unto the other." Between the Christian Sabbath and the first Sabbath of the world there is no difference save the change of day, which was effected by the authority of Christ, and agreed with the general method of redemption. It was a case of putting new wine into new vessels. "How pied would Christianity have looked if it had worn a coat all new in other respects, but had had on the shirt or piecing of the old Sabbath! And how unfit was it to have tied Christians to the observation of the old Sabbath of the Jews!" With a few observations on the fitness of making Christ's resurrection, rather than the original creation, the subject of sabbatic commemoration, the sermon closes. The learned Lightfoot, immersed in his rabbinic researches, discussed the Sabbath with slight reference to the practical questions, which in the first place would demand the attention of less academic thinkers; but it seemed well to consider his views, as indicating the mental attitude of a really considerable divine. Less erudite, but by no means less gifted with intellect, a man immersed in the politics of the time, compelled to bring his theories to the touchstone of human life as it proceeds among ordinary folk, a preacher of righteousness, and an exemplary parish priest, RICHARD BAXTER may be taken as the exponent of sane and tolerant Puritanism. In his voluminous writings the Sabbatarian controversy looms largely, and perhaps there is no more satisfying discussion of the subject, from the Puritan standpoint, to be found in the immense literature produced on either side of the question than his treatise on *The Divine Appointment of the Lord's Day*,[1] published in 1671, but embodying the experience and the teaching of the earlier period, when Baxter was in the front of political movements. He explains his object in a short Preface, which throws a curious light on the age. "The reason of my writing it," he says, "was the necessity and request of some very upright, godly persons, who are lately fallen into doubt or error in point of the Sabbath Day, conceiving that, because the fourth commandment was written in stone, it was wholly unchangeable, and consequently the Seventh-day Sabbath in force, and that the Lord's day is not a day separated by God to holy worship." He adds, not without a touch of gentle

---

[1] The treatise is printed in vol. xiii. of Orme's edition of *Baxter's Practical Works*, pp. 364–466.

sarcasm: "I much pity and wonder at those godly men, who are so much for stretching the words of Scripture, to a sense that other men cannot find in them, as that in the words 'Graven Images' in the second commandment, they can find all set forms of prayer, all composed, studied sermons, and all things about worship of man's invention to be images and idolatry; and yet they cannot find the abrogation of the Jewish Sabbath in the express words of Colossians ii. 16, nor the other texts which I have cited; nor can they find the institution of the Lord's day in all the texts and evidences produced for it." He then states with less than his usual diffusiveness—a result, perhaps, of the separation from his books which he laments in the Preface—the familiar arguments for disallowing the Jewish law while retaining a moral obligation on Christians to observe one day in seven, and justifying the observance of the Lord's Day on the ground of Apostolic appointment under special inspiration of the Holy Spirit. Throughout he keeps up a running criticism of Peter Heylyn's *History of the Sabbath*, published in 1636, which represented the extreme ecclesiastical theory of the origin and obligation of the Lord's Day. Then he deals with various questions raised by the Sabbatarians. He decides the contested point as to the precise limits of the sacred day by the sensible observation that the common estimation of the country where one lives will best answer the ends of the institution.[1] He insists on the public exercises of religion as peculiarly binding on the Christian;[2] and, in this view, he certainly represented the main stream of Puritan teaching. Dr. Gardiner does not seem to me justified when he describes the Puritan view of the Sabbath as merely individualistic.[3] In its ultimate principle this may have been the case, but certainly not in conscious thought, still less in accepted theory. Dr. Bound, the protagonist of Sabbatarianism, had insisted on the duty of attending at sermons, and Baxter, who was, hardly less than his Anglican contemporaries, wont to seek his conception of Lord's Day observance in the practice of the primitive Christians, never wearies of enforcing the social character of the day. He insists on the consecration of the entire day. "So much of the day as can be spared from public church worship (and diversions of necessity) should be next spent most in holy family-exercises."[4] Always, however, private and family devotions are to yield place to the public worship, because for the latter the Lord's

---

[1] *Ibid.*, p. 428.

[2] *Ibid.*, p. 429. "The principal work of the day is the communion of Christians in the public exercise of God's worship."

[3] *History of England*, vol. iii. p. 247.

[4] *Loc. cit.*, p. 433.

Day is principally set apart.[1] To the not unnatural objection that human nature is not equal to the strain of such continuous exercises, Baxter replies only with severe rebukes of the cold-heartedness implied in so regarding the worship of God. Having dealt with the duties, he then discusses the more common abuses of the day: and here he falls foul of the common Sunday recreations, which had originally caused so much disturbance. All the intense Puritanism of the man comes out as he denounces, with prophetic fervour, amusements which he had learned, as a parish priest, to recognise as the ministers of sin. He appeals to the recollections and experiences of his own life. "I cannot forget when my conscience was against their courses, and called me to better things, how hardly when I was young, I passed by the dancing and the playing congregations, and especially when in the passage I must bear their scorn. And I was one year a schoolmaster, and found how hard it was for the poor children to avoid such snares, even when they were sure to be whipped the next day for their pleasures. . . ."[2]

"I cannot forget that in my youth in those late times, when we lost the labours of some of our conformable godly teachers for not reading publicly the Book of Sports and Dancing on the Lord's-days,

---
[1] p. 435.   [2] p. 443.

one of my father's own tenants was the town-piper, hired by the year (for many years together), and the place of the dancing-assembly was not a hundred yards from our door, and we could not on the Lord's-day either read a chapter, or pray, or sing a psalm, or catechise, or instruct a servant, but with the noise of the pipe and tabor, and the shouting in the street, continually in our ears; and even among a tractable people we were the common scorn of all the rabble in the streets, and called Puritans, Precisians, and Hypocrites, because we rather chose to read the Scriptures than to do as they did (though there was no savour of Nonconformity in our family). And when the people by the book were allowed to play and dance out of public service-time, they could so hardly break off their sports, that many a time the reader was fain to stay till the piper and players would give over; and sometimes the morrice-dancers would come into the church in all the linen and scarfs, and antic dresses, with morice-bells jingling at their legs. And as soon as common-prayer was read, did haste out presently to their play again."[1] He will not allow the plea that labourers at least might have a valid claim to Sunday amusements. "Is it their bodies or their minds that need recreation?" he asks very cogently, and

---

[1] p. 444.

turns the tables on the objectors by saying that if bodily recreations were needed by labourers, landlords might abate to their tenants as much rent as one day's vacancy from labour in a month or a fortnight will amount to. Students, lawyers, ministers, and gentlemen, who work with their brains, can for the most part obtain their bodily recreations during the week. To the contention that the mind is incapable, without some change, of the protracted concentration on worship which his theory demands, Baxter answers that there is ample variety in the differing exercises of religion, and that the true origin of the alleged mental fatigue is lack of love. "Come and spend but a day in loving God, as thou dost in talking of Him, and try whether love, and the holiest love, be a wearisome work." He interposes a pointed appeal to the clergy, then as now heavily accused of dulness in the pulpit. "But I will tell them that are the teachers of the people, an honester way to cure the people's weariness, than to send them to a piper or to a play to cure it. Preach with such life and awakening seriousness, preach with such grateful, holy eloquence, and with such easy method, and with such variety of wholesome matter, that the people may never be weary of you."[1] Of course the inevitable Calvin has to be reckoned with. His

---
[1] p. 448.

Sunday game was a godsend to the Sabbath-breakers. Baxter's answer is both ingenious and interesting. "You must remember," he says, "that they" (*i.e.* the foreign reformers) "came newly out of popery, and had seen the Lord's day, and a superabundance of other human holy days imposed on the churches to be ceremoniously observed, and they did not all of them, so clearly as they ought, discern the difference between the Lord's day, and those holy days, or church festivals, and so did too promiscuously conjoin them in their reproofs of the burdens imposed on the Church." . . . "And for Calvin you must know that he spent every day so like to a Lord's day . . . that he might the more easier be tempted to make the less difference in his judgment between the Lord's day and other days. . . . But as England hath been the happiest in this piece of reformation, so all men are inexcusable that encourage idleness, sensuality, or neglect of the important duties of the day."[1]

Baxter proceeds to discuss "What things should not be scrupled as unlawful on the Lord's day," and in the course of his discussion shows some pretty play as a casuist. He concedes the lawfulness of taking exercise for the sake of one's health, and confesses to doing so himself, but privately, lest he should tempt others to sin.[2]

---
[1] p. 451.   [2] p. 457.

Even the modified Sabbatarianism of Richard Baxter has an impracticable and even extravagant aspect now; but then it commended itself to the strong intelligence and healthy moral sense of men like Sir Matthew Hale, who adopted it for themselves, and confessed its value for mind and body, as well as spirit. And even now the reflection may sometimes occur to us, as we mark on all hands, and feel in ourselves, the injury of that severe and ever severer strain of modern life, as it proceeds in our great cities, that there was a deeper reasonableness in the Puritan practice than the arbitrary and whimsical arguments, by which they often defended it, might at first view suggest. In repudiating, as we cannot but repudiate, the bondage of the Puritan Sabbath, we may well admit a certain anxiety, lest we shall have endangered that strength and simplicity of the Puritan character, which depended more than we suspect on the normal severity of a religious habit.

The Presbyterian Experiment

However opinions may vary as to the intrinsic worth of the Laudian theory of the English Church, and as to the character of the Laudian ecclesiastics who strove to reduce that theory to practice, there can be but one opinion as to the effect produced on the public opinion of the country at the time. The extreme unpopularity of the English hierarchy after a few years of Laudian supremacy is equally certain, and, at first sight, hard to explain. The bishops were for the most part personally respectable, and there is no reason for thinking that their administration of the Church was—judged by the standard of their time—exceptionally harsh or unjust. The ecclesiastical courts were, no doubt, unpopular with those who came within their grasp, and they were probably no more free from corruption than other courts; but even in that age, when the criminal category included classes of offenders which have long ceased to be the concern of the law, the actual number of persons who had private reasons for disliking the ecclesiastical system cannot have been

FEELING AGAINST THE BISHOPS

relatively so considerable as to affect in such an absolute way the general sentiment of the nation.

It is sufficiently evident that the intimate association of the hierarchy with the secular government prejudiced it badly in the judgment of that great section of the people which resented, and in the end resisted, the unconstitutional course which the secular government took under the earlier Stuarts. Men carried over to the credit of the hierarchy the suspicion and dislike with which the political action of the leading bishops had filled them; and the confusion was facilitated by the personal character of Archbishop Laud. Nothing was too petty or too apparently remote from spiritual interests for his interference.[1] His clear-cut personality met men's eyes at every turn; his sharp speeches were rankling in many minds. His zeal for those unaccustomed ceremonies which in his eyes were the expressions and bulwarks of religion, but in the

---

[1] *Cf.* Fuller's description of Archbishop Whitgift, who "repaired daily to the Council table early in the morning, and, after his usual appreciation of a 'good-morrow' to the lords, he requested to know if there were any Church business to be debated, and, if the answer were returned in the affirmative, he stayed and attended the issue of the matter. But if no such matter appeared, he craved leave to be dispensed withal, saying, 'Then, my lords, here is no need of me,' and departed: a commendable practice, clearing himself from all aspersions of civil pragmaticalness and tending much to the just support of his reputation" (*v. Church History, sub anno* 1589).

eyes of the average Englishman were no better than illegal and superstitious follies, his astonishing pertinacity and ubiquitousness, even his personal piety (always semi-grotesque in English eyes)—all combined to constitute him in the eyes of the people the incarnation of the Caroline tyranny in Church and State. It is an error to suppose that Laud was only disliked by the Puritans, and to discount the suggestions of his remarkable unpopularity by their not altogether disinterested prejudices. The fiercest denunciation possible came from men who, under ordinary circumstances, would have stood by those in authority. HARBOTLE GRIMSTON, for example, a country gentleman of the respectable Conservative type, "the very embodiment of a constitutional Conservative," to borrow Mr. Shaw's description, used language about the Archbishop which could only come from an intense repugnance.

"Mr. Speaker," he said, "we are now fallen upon the great man, the Archbishop of Canterbury; look upon him as he is in highness, and he is the sty of all pestilential filth that hath infested the State and Government of this Commonwealth; look upon him in his dependencies, and he is the only man, the only man that hath raised and advanced all those that, together with himself, have been the authors and causers of all our ruins, miseries, and calamities we now groan under. . . . Who is it,

Mr. Speaker, but this great Archbishop of Canterbury, that hath sat at the helm, to steer and manage all the projects that have been set on foot in this kingdom this last ten years past? and rather than he would stand out, he hath most unworthily trucked and chaffered in the meanest of them. . . . Mr. Speaker, he hath been the great and common enemy of all goodness and good men, and it is not safe that such a viper should be near His Majesty's person to distil his poison into his sacred ears."[1]

This was the language, be it remembered, of one who was, and was considered, a moderate man. The dislike of Laud always seemed in some degree personal to the man himself, but dislike, hardly less vehement, was expressed against the whole episcopal system. When the great London petition against Episcopacy, signed by no less than 15,000 persons, and presented to the House by as many as 1,600 gentlemen of quality, was discussed, very remarkable speeches were made by the champions of the bishops. Lord DIGBY, for example, began an extremely eloquent oration with the declaration that there was no man within the walls of Parliament more sensible of the heavy grievance of Church government than himself, "nor whose affections were keener to the clipping of these wings of the prelates, whereby they have mounted to such

---

[1] Rushworth, iv. p. 122.

insolencies, nor whose zeal was more ardent to the searing them so, as they may never spring again."

"I do not think," he said, "that any people hath been ever more provoked than the generality of England of late years by the insolencies and exorbitances of the prelates.

"I protest sincerely, Mr. Speaker, I cannot cast mine eye upon this petition, nor my thoughts on the practices of the churchmen, that have governed it of late, but they appeared to me as a scourge employed by God upon us for the sins of the nation; and I could not but think of that passage in the Book of Kings, 'He that escapes the sword of Hazael shall Jehu slay, and he that escapes Jehu shall Elisha slay.'

"Methinks the vengeance of the prelates hath been so laid, as if 'twere meant, no generation, no degree, no complection of mankind should escape it.

"Was there a man of nice and tender conscience? Him have they afflicted with scandal, in Adiaphoris, imposing on him those things as necessary, which he thinks unlawful, and they themselves knew to be but indifferent.

"Was there a man of legal conscience, that made the establishment by law, the measure of his religion? Him have they nettled with innovations, with fresh introductions of Popery.

"Was there a man of meek and humble spirit? Him have they trampled to dirt in their pride.

"Was there a man of a proud and arrogant nature? Him have they bereft of reason, with indignation at their superlative insolence about him.

"Was there a man peaceably affected, studious of the quiet and tranquillity of his country? Their incendiaryships hath plagued him.

"Was there a man faithfully addicted to the right of the crown, loyally affected to the king's supremacy? How hath he been galled by their new Oath? A direct covenant against it.

"Was there a man tenacious of the liberty and property of the subject? Have they not set forth books, or sermons, or canons destructive to them all?

"Was there a man of a pretty sturdy conscience that would not blanch for a little? This pernicious oath has made him sensible and wounded; or, I fear, prepared him for the devil.

"Was there a man that durst mutter against their insolencies? He may inquire for his lugs; they have been within the bishop's visitation; as if they would not only derive their brandishment of the spiritual sword from St. Peter, but of the material one too, and the right to cut off ears.

"Mr. Speaker, as dully, as faintly, as unlively, as

in language, these actions of the prelates hath been expressed unto you; I am confident there is no man hears me, but is brimful of indignation.

"For my part, I profess, I am so inflamed with the sense of them, that I find myself ready to cry out with the loudest of the fifteen thousand: 'Down with them, down with them, even to the ground.'"

Lord Digby was defending Episcopacy; he follows up this tremendous denunciation of the bishops by a vigorous and telling argument against attributing to the institution the faults of individuals. He was a man of the world, and, beyond most of his hearers, had personal knowledge of foreign countries. He knew that there might be worse tyranny than that of bishops. "If we hearken to those that would quite extirpate Episcopacy: I am confident that instead of every bishop we put down in a diocese, we shall set up a pope in every parish." The speech from which we have quoted was no impromptu utterance; it bears all the marks of careful preparation. Its conclusion was a declaration of policy: "Let us not destroy bishops, but make bishops such as they were in the primitive times. Do their large territories, their large revenues offend? Let them be retrenched; the good Bishop of Hippo had but a narrow diocese. Do their courts and subordinates offend? Let them be brought to govern, as in the primitive times, by assemblies of their clergy. Doth their intermeddling in secular affairs offend? Exclude them from the capacity: it is no more than what reason and all antiquity hath interdicted them." The orator's political judgment was sounder than his knowledge of ecclesiastical history; the significant thing about the speech is the open admission that the Laudian administration was incapable of defence. Perhaps even more suggestive is the speech of Lord FALKLAND in the same debate: for Lord Falkland was free from the opportunist element which was certainly present in the character of Lord Digby. He deservedly bore the reputation of a just, unprejudiced, outspoken man of exceptionable gifts and learning. His speech has the ring of sincerity, and we may accept it as a faithful version of the opinion of the cultivated class on the situation. The opening sentence strikes the keynote of severe yet discriminating censure, which is sustained throughout: "Mr. Speaker, he is a great stranger in Israel who knows not this kingdom hath long laboured under many and great oppressions, both in Religion and Liberty: and his acquaintance here is not great, or his ingenuity less, who doth not both know and acknowledge that a great, if not a principal, cause of both these have been some bishops and their adherents.

"Mr. Speaker, a little search will serve to find out

them to have been the destruction of unity, under pretence of uniformity: to have brought in superstition and scandal under the titles of reverence and decency: to have defiled our church by adorning our churches: to have slackened the strictness of that union which was formerly between us, and those of our religion beyond the sea, an action as unpolitic as ungodly. . . .

"The truth is, Mr. Speaker, That as some ill Ministers in our State first took away our money from us, and after endeavoured to make our money not worth the taking, by turning it into brass by a kind of Anti-philosopher's stone: so these men used us in the point of preaching; first, depressing it to their power, and next labouring to make it such, as the harm had not been much if it had been depressed: the most frequent subjects even in the most sacred auditories, being the *Jus Divinum* of bishops, and tithes, the sacredness of the clergy, the sacrilege of impropriations, the demolishing of Puritanism and propriety, the building of the Prerogative at Paul's, the introduction of such doctrines, as, admitting them true, the truth would not recompense the scandal: or such as were so far false, that, as Sir Thomas More says of the Casuists, their business was not to keep men from sinning, but to confirm them ... . so it seemed their work was to try how much of a papist might be brought in without popery : and to destroy as much as they could of the Gospel, without bringing themselves into danger of being destroyed by the Law.

"Mr. Speaker, To go yet further, some of them have so industriously laboured to deduce themselves from Rome, that they have given great suspicion that in gratitude they desire to return thither, or at least to meet it half way : some have evidently laboured to bring in an English, though not a Roman, Popery : I mean not only the outside and dress of it, but, equally absolute, a blind dependence of the people upon the clergy, and of the clergy upon themselves : and have opposed the Papacy beyond the seas, that they might settle one beyond the water :[1] nay, common fame is more than ordinarily false, if none of them have found a way to reconcile the opinions of Rome to the preferments of England : and to be so absolutely, directly, and cordially Papists, that it is all that Fifteen hundred pounds a year can do to keep them from confessing it." Falkland dilates in this strain at some length, and concludes by endorsing Digby's proposals. He thinks an Episcopate, stripped of its temporal functions, associated with the inferior clergy in the exercise of its spiritual office, and partially dis-

---

[1] *i.e.*, across the Thames, at Lambeth. The orator was speaking in Westminster.

endowed, will certainly be incapable of grave mischiefs and might even be serviceable.

"My opinion is, That we should not root up this ancient tree, as dead as it appears, till we have tried whether by this, or the like lopping of the branches, the sap which was unable to feed the whole, may not serve to make what is left both grow and flourish."[1]

Such speeches by such men seem to me to constitute weightier evidence against the Laudian hierarchy than the language of the numerous and numerously signed petitions, which from all sides poured into the Parliament, giving lists of grievances and clamouring for the destruction of the episcopal system; for the hand of the not unpractised agitator is very apparent in those petitions, and while they illustrate the general discontent of the nation, I should hesitate to build much on their specific statements. Men signed what was put before them, and, sometimes, if Clarendon speaks truly,[2] what

---

[1] Rushworth, iv. pp. 170–87.

[2] v. *History of the Rebellion*, vol. i. p. 271 [Oxford, 1888]. "It was a strange uningenuity and mountebankery that was practised in the procuring those petitions, which continued ever after in the like addresses. The course was, first, to prepare a petition, very modest and dutiful for the form, and for the matter not very unreasonable: and to communicate it at some public meeting, where care was taken it should be received with approbation: the subscription of very few hands filled the paper

STATE OF OPINION IN 1640

they signed was not always identical with what went up to Parliament. But the speeches which we have quoted were those of the least fanatical and best informed public men of the time, uttered under circumstances, which called for reserve and deliberately designed in the interest of the episcopal system.

Mr. Shaw, in his admirable history of this period, has shown that when the Long Parliament met in November, 1640, there was no great volume of opinion hostile to Episcopacy as such. Probably the general view was that expressed in the House by all the members, whose speeches have been preserved, that there had been scandalous abuse of episcopal power, that drastic reforms both in the extent and in the manner of exercising that power were necessary, but that the power itself should be

---

itself where the petition was written, and therefore many more sheets were annexed, for the reception of the number which gave all the credit and procured all the countenance to the undertaking. When a multitude of hands was procured, the petition itself was cut off and a new one framed suitable to the design in hand, and annexed to the long list of names which were subscribed to the former. And by this means many men found their names subscribed to petitions of which they before had never heard."

Mr. Shaw has examined this allegation and shown that Clarendon has put an unfair interpretation on procedure which "seems to me [Mr. S.] to be perfectly legitimate"— (*v. History of the English Church*, 1640–1660, p. 23, note).

retained. Very soon, however, the cry for reformation was exchanged for the demand for abolition. Presbyterian opinions had never, since the Reformation, been wholly unrepresented among the Anglican clergy. As early as the year 1568 we are assured by Fuller that there was a " generation of active and zealous nonconformists " who inveighed against the Church discipline, "accounting every thing from Rome which was not from Geneva, endeavouring in all things to conform the government of the English Church to the Presbyterian Reformation."[1] Of these men, Thomas Cartwright was the leader, and they certainly commanded considerable influence. The attempt was made, and persisted in for some while, to set up the Presbyterian polity within the framework of the episcopal system. In 1572 a presbytery was actually set up at Wandsworth, which, in Fuller's words, "was the first-born of all presbyteries in England, and *secundum usum Wandsworth* as much honoured by some as *secundum usum Sarum* by others." The character of this extraordinary attempt to quietly transform an episcopal into a presbyterian Church has been very well described by the present Bishop of Oxford, in his excellent *Introduction to the Fifth Book of Hooker's Ecclesiastical Polity*. The calling and election of

---

[1] *v. Church History, sub anno* 1568.

ministers was to be secured by requiring that no man should offer himself to the ministry, and that, when anyone was called by a Church, he should impart it to the *classis*, or conference, of which he was a member, and then, if approved by that body, be commended to the bishop for ordination. The office of *elders* was to be provided for by arranging that men likely to act as elders should be elected as churchwardens. *Deacons*, in the Puritan sense of the title, were to be got by taking similar care in regard to the election of collectors for the poor. The periodical assemblies of *classes* (or conferences) and *provincial*, *comitial*, and *national synods* were to be arranged by "a distribution of all churches, according to the rules set down in the synodical discipline." The extension of the system was to be advanced by the *classes* dealing earnestly with patrons to present fit men. Thus, at point after point, the Genevan system was to be pushed forward in the Established Church, and the forms of the Church bent as near as might be to the Genevan type. This was to be done by men who were holding office in the Church; and it was agreed that "those ceremonies in the Book of Common Prayer, which being taken from popery are in controversy, ought to be omitted, if it may be done without danger of being put from the ministry; but if there be imminent danger of being deprived, then let the matter be communicated to the *classis* in which that church is, to be determined by them."[1]

This does not seem to us a very ingenuous course of action, but probably it seemed more legitimate in the sixteenth century than it does in the twentieth. The vigour of Archbishop Whitgift stamped out this nascent Presbyterianism, and, though no doubt a certain number of the clergy cherished a preference for that type of ecclesiastical polity, there seems little reason to suppose that any organised Presbyterian party existed in England until the course of public events brought the Presbyterianism of Scotland prominently before

---

[1] Fuller states the actual situation with his usual felicity. "The condition of the English Church must be conceived sad, which at the same time had two disciplines, both of them pleading scripture and primitive practice, each striving to support itself, and suppress its rival: the Hierarchy commanded by authority, established by law, confirmed by general practice, and continued so long by custom in this land, that, had one at this time lived the age of Methuselah, he could not remember the beginning thereof in Britain. The Presbytery, though wanting the stamp of authority, claiming to be the purer metal, founded by some clergymen, favoured by many of the gentry, and followed by more of the common sort, who, being prompted by that natural principle—that the weakest side must be most watchful, what they wanted in strength they supplied in activity: but what won them most repute was their ministers' painful preaching in populous places: it being observed in England that those who hold the helm of the pulpit always steer people's hearts as they please" (book ix. 21–3).

the English people, and that under circumstances eminently calculated to commend it to their approval.

The first effective check to the King's career of unconstitutional absolutism was given in Scotland on the very matter, about which Laud's proceedings in England had set men thinking. The attempt to force Episcopacy on the Scots was the crowning act of a policy of uniformity in the Church, conceived in the interest of the hierarchy and carried through by the reckless use of prerogative. And Laud himself, with the curious fatuity which marked his whole attitude towards public sentiment, was the prominent agent in the policy, of which he was universally believed to be the author. It followed inevitably that all who, for whatever reason, hated and dreaded Laud—and they were many—thought the worse of Episcopacy for his advocacy of its claims, and the better of Presbyterianism for defeating him. Under the Laudian administration, Episcopacy became generally suspected of inherent incompatibility with Protestantism, and this happened when Protestantism was fighting a desperate battle against the forces of the counter-Reformation. Only eight years had passed since Gustavus Adolphus had fallen on the field of Lützen (1632), and Englishmen glowed with shame to reflect that in that holy war, which the heroic Swede had personified, England stood aside in an ignoble and unnatural inaction. The revulsion against the bishops is only intelligible when it is seen how utterly out of touch with the national feeling they had come to be, or, at least, to appear. The heroes of the time were all non-episcopalian. At the crisis of the conflict for truth and liberty the cause of God owed nothing to the bishops. Might it not be the case— so men inevitably reflected—that those more ardent and thorough-going Reformers of Scotland and the Continent were wiser, as well as more logical, when they swept away the whole ancient fabric of episcopal order? Dr. Masson estimated that when the Long Parliament met in 1640, among the parish clergy "as many as 1,000 or 1,500 of the more extreme Puritans were considered as either belonging to the [anti-episcopal party], or convertible to it by circumstances." "But," he says, "among the laity it was enormously and growingly powerful. Not without a sprinkling among the nobility and wealthier gentry, it had a large number of adherents among the minor gentry, while in the great body of the people it counted its tens of thousands. London was its stronghold and headquarters, the traditional Puritanism of that city having now almost avowedly taken the form of a frenzy for Presbyterianism. Most of the other considerable towns were centres of the same feeling, and there were particular counties, more especially the eastern counties of Essex, Suffolk, Cambridge, Huntingdon, and Bedford, and the north-western counties of Lancaster and Chester, where Root-and-Branch principles were distinctly predominant among the farmers and tenantry."[1] From the beginning of the constitutional conflict there had been a good understanding between the Scots and the Parliamentary leaders. When, after the King's defeat in the second "Bishops' War," the negotiations for peace were transferred, at the request of the victors, from Ripon to London, the Scotch Commissioners were accompanied by some Presbyterian divines, who were both eager to seize the opportunity for spreading their principles and eminently qualified to do so with effect. By a striking coincidence the Scotch preachers and the Earl of Strafford entered London on the same day. The Commissioners were received with the utmost consideration, lodged in the city, and sumptuously entertained. The house assigned to them joined hard to St. Antholin's Church, into which there was a private passage, and there they preached with great success.

Clarendon's account is, as usual, disfigured by prejudice, but it is a lively description of the facts notwithstanding. He says that Alexander Hender-

---

[1] *v. Life of John Milton*, vol. ii. p. 200.

son was the principal preacher, and that to hear those sermons "there was so great a conflux and resort, by the citizens out of humour and faction, by others of all quality out of curiosity, and by some that they might the better justify the contempt they had of them, that, from the first appearance of day in the morning on every Sunday to the shutting in of the light, the church was never empty, they (especially the women) who had the happiness to get into the church in the morning (they who could not hang upon or about the windows without, to be auditors or spectators) keeping their places till the afternoon's exercise was finished, which both morning and afternoon, except to palates and appetites ridiculously corrupted, was the most insipid and flat that could be delivered upon any deliberation."[1]

Clarendon was no fair judge of Scotch preachers or of Presbyterian logic, but we may be sure that, however eloquent the one, or cogent the other, neither would have, by itself, overcome the English dislike of "covenants," and it must be added, English prejudice against those who then, and for long afterwards, were accounted foreigners. The acceptance of Presbyterianism by the English Parliament three years later was the price paid for Scotch assistance, when the success of the royal

---

[1] *History of the Rebellion*, vol. i. p. 251. [Oxford, 1888.]

arms had made it apparent that without such assistance the King would prevail; and, so soon as the defeat of the King was assured, Presbyterianism was quietly dropped by the Government and eagerly repudiated by the nation. As we review the course of events we can see that a curious interchange of parts had taken place. The enforcement of religious uniformity throughout Great Britain had become the object, no more of Laud, already half-forgotten in the Tower, which he would only leave in order to mount the scaffold, but of Laud's late victims and present masters. Alexander Henderson was a more generous and liberal man than the Archbishop, but he was deluded by the same error. His idea was, says his Scotch biographer, "to effect a presbyterian uniformity, not only in the worship of the three kingdoms, but in that of all the reformed churches. In this he was guided by motives pure and patriotic. He not only resisted the aims of the King to enforce prelatic uniformity in our church, but he accompanied the Scottish army across the Tweed, and struggled to compel the English to presbyterian conformity."[1]

Step by step the Long Parliament was driven by the goad of apparent necessity first to abandon its

---

[1] *Life and Times of Alexander Henderson*, by John Aiton, D.D., p. 451. [Edinburgh, 1836.]

original purpose of reforming the episcopal system, then, to abolish that system altogether, finally, to accept the Solemn League and Covenant, and the system, with certain modifications, which it presupposed.

The year 1643 was full of disasters to the Parliamentary cause. A series of Royalist victories culminating in Rupert's storming of Bristol reduced the Parliament to seek the aid of the Scots, and, since that aid could be obtained on no other terms, to accept the Covenant. Already the famous "Assembly of Divines" was established at Westminster, summoned originally to form a permanent Board of Advice to Parliament in all matters affecting religion, and destined to do work of lasting importance, and to take rank as one of the most illustrious "sacred synods" of history. The Assembly consisted of thirty-two lay-assessors and one hundred and twenty-five divines, including the Scottish commissioners, to one of whom, the lively and ardent, but garrulous and conceited, Baillie, we owe a curious and interesting account of the proceedings. Not all the divines who were summoned attended, for the King had by proclamation prohibited attendance, and his authority was respected by the Episcopalians. On the opening day, July 1st, 1643, only sixty-nine divines were present, and, generally, the attendance appears to have ranged between sixty and eighty. Every member on taking his seat had to make the following declaration :- –

"I, ——, do seriously promise and vow, in the presence of Almighty God, that in this Assembly, whereof I am a member, I will maintain nothing in point of doctrine but what I believe to be most agreeable to the Word of God : nor in point of discipline, but what I shall conceive to conduce most to the glory of God, and the good and peace of His Church." Every Monday morning the protestation was read afresh. Among the members was Dr. JOHN LIGHTFOOT, who kept a journal of the proceedings, from which I extract the following account of the taking of the Covenant :—

"*Friday, September 22nd.*—Before we got out of the Abbey, we had word to return to our House again, for the Parliament had something to impart unto us : which at last came by the hand of Mr. Salloway, namely, 'that the Lords and Commons intended to take the Covenant on Monday, in St. Margaret's, Westminster, and sent to us to do the like : and that we should appoint some to pray at the time, and some to give a word of exhortation, which we did accordingly, and nominated Mr. White, the assessor, to pray before, Mr. Nye to make the exhortation, and Dr. Gouge to pray after.

"*Monday, September 25th.*—This morning being

met, we had word presently, after our sitting into Assembly, that the House of Commons was gone to St. Margaret's Church, and so we went after them. And after a psalm given by Mr. Wilson, picking several verses, to suit the present occasion, out of several psalms, Mr. White prayed near upon an hour. Then he came down out of the pulpit, and Mr. Nye went up, and made an exhortation of another hour long. After he had done, Mr. Henderson, out of the seat where he sat, did the like: and all tended to forward the covenant. Then Mr. Nye, being in the pulpit still, read the covenant: and, at every clause of it, the House of Commons, and we of the Assembly lift up our hands, and gave our consent thereby to it, and then went all into the chancel, and subscribed our hands: and afterward we had a prayer by Dr. Gouge, and another psalm by Mr. Wilson, and departed into the Assembly again; and after prayer, adjourned till Thursday morning, because of the fast.

"*Friday, September* 29*th.*—Being sat, we hasted to adjourn, that we might go hear a sermon at St. Margaret's. For all the lords, knights, gentlemen, Scots, divines, and soldiers, which were now in London, and not inhabitants there, took the covenant: and Mr. Coleman by an order preached to them."[1]

---
[1] Lightfoot, *Works*, vol. xiii. pp. 15, 16.

The Covenant was taken in all the London churches on the following Sunday, and ordered to be taken throughout the kingdom with all convenient expedition. This famous document, thus, so far as the Parliament could secure that result, bound upon the English people, was composed by Alexander Henderson, and in one or two phrases[1] modified in deference to English objections. It consists of six clauses with a preamble and a conclusion. The salient pledges are those of the first and second clauses. The Covenanters "all subscribe, and each one of us for himself, with our hands lifted up to the most High God, do swear,—

"I. That we shall sincerely, really, and constantly, through the grace of God, endeavour, in our several places and callings, the preservation of the reformed religion in the Church of Scotland, in doctrine, worship, discipline, and government, against our enemies: the reformation of religion in the kingdoms of England and Ireland, in doctrine, worship, discipline, and government, *according to the Word of God, and the example of the best reformed Churches;* and shall endeavour to bring the Churches of God in the three kingdoms to the nearest conjunction and uniformity in religion, Confession of faith, Form of Church Government, Directory for Worship and Catechising: that we, and our posterity

---

[1] I have italicised these.

after us, may, as brethren, live in faith and love, and the Lord may delight to dwell in the midst of us.

"II. That we shall, in like manner, without respect of persons, endeavour the extirpation of Popery, Prelacy (*that is, Church government by archbishops, bishops, their chancellors and commissaries, deans, deans and chapters, archdeacons, and all ecclesiastical officers depending on that hierarchy*), superstition, heresy, schism, profaneness, and whatsoever shall be found contrary to sound doctrine and the power of godliness: lest we partake in other men's sins, and thereby be in danger to receive of their plagues: and that the Lord may be one, and His name one, in the three kingdoms."

The third clause pledged the Covenanters "to preserve and defend the King's Majesty's person and authority, in the preservation and defence of the true religion and liberties of the kingdom"; and protested that they "had no thoughts or intentions to diminish his Majesty's just power and greatness." At the time this declaration of loyalty had an aspect of gratuitous hypocrisy which naturally incensed both the King himself and his supporters, but its sincerity was made manifest at a later period, when the rise of the Independents overwhelmed both Crown and Covenanters in a common calamity, and the restoration of the monarchy, when at last it was effected, was mainly the work of Presbyterians.

The Solemn League and Convenant, as it was subscribed in England, was, as we have said, an amended document, representing in its slight but significant amendments the latent repugnance of the English mind to so severe an ecclesiastical system as that of Scotland. "In the first draft of the Covenant, as agreed upon at Edinburgh, Vane had proposed an amendment by adding after the words, 'the Church of Scotland in doctrine, worship, discipline, and government,' the words, 'according to the word of God.' When the Covenant was referred to the Assembly of Divines at Westminster, this amendment was retained, along with another of the Assembly's own, defining the prelacy, which it was desired to abolish, as that which consisted in archbishops, bishops, etc. The scope of both amendments is plain. The former would pledge the Covenanted Parliament to the Scottish system only in so far as it was found agreeable to the Word of God : the latter gave it freedom in the construction it put upon the word 'prelacy'— in the view it took of the then existing Church system. Practically both amendments were retained in the final form of the Covenant."[1]

---

[1] *History of the English Church* 1640–1660, by W. A. Shaw, vol. I. p. 143.

The situation, then, in September, 1643, was distinctly complicated. The ancient ecclesiastical system of the country had been overthrown by Parliamentary Ordinance, and nothing had as yet been set up in its place. The Assembly of Divines was in session at Westminster, charged to draft and recommend to Parliament a constitution for the English Church. Under the pressure of political exigency, the Parliament had accepted the Covenant, and thus "had forfeited its future freedom of action in the matter of Church reform," but, in the process, had endeavoured to retain a measure of liberty with respect to Church order.[1] The Scotch Commissioners were in London pressing forward with fervent zeal, and no less astuteness, the complete establishment in England of the Presbyterian system of Scotland, but both in Parliament and in the Assembly there were very apparent signs of restiveness. Erastians and Independents, from opposite standpoints, were averse to Presbyterianism; and

---

[1] Baxter states this clearly enough: "The Synod stumbled at some things in it, and especially at the word 'prelacy.' . . . Hereupon grew some debate in the Assembly, some being against every degree of Bishops (especially the Scottish Divines), and others being for a moderate Episcopacy. But these English Divines would not subscribe the Covenant till there were an alteration suited to their judgments; and so a parenthesis was yielded to, as describing that sort of Prelacy which they opposed" (*Autobiography*, i. pp. 48, 49).

there certainly was in the country a great volume of opinion, not as yet audible, which disliked the total extirpation of Episcopacy, and desired rather the adoption of some such modified episcopal system as that proposed by Archbishop Ussher. Meanwhile, the war was in progress, and the men, who were shaping the ecclesiastical constitution, were preoccupied with the primary task of crushing the King. Hence the interplay of spiritual and secular motives which everywhere reveals itself in the proceedings of Parliament. The Westminster Assembly is dragged, not without reluctance and even protest, in the wake of political movements. Baillie's letters present a curious but not unfamiliar blending of ecclesiastical fervour and political cunning. Milton was not far from the facts when he wrote of "plots and packing worse than those of Trent" as proceeding in the Assembly of Divines. The prestige of the Assembly steadily sank as it slowly worked through its immense programme of business, and, by the time the complete Presbyterian polity was ready to be set up, the nation was weary of it.

Mr. Shaw discusses the constructive work of the Westminster Assembly under nine heads, which we can here do little more than enumerate. They are: (1) *The Thirty-nine Articles*. The Assembly revised the first fifteen only. (2) *Church Government*. In the protracted debates on this subject two factors came into prominence—the alienation of the Independents and the political pressure from Scotland. In the course of the years 1645–6 Parliament substantially agreed upon the Presbyterian system. (3) *Presbyterian Jurisdiction or Discipline.* When it is remembered how vehement had been the complaints of the Puritans against the lax discipline of the bishops,[1] it will be seen that this was a point of cardinal importance. " The essence of Presbyterianism is discipline." When the whole system of the medieval Church, disciplinary as well as liturgical, had been swept away, some substitute was required, and this was provided by courts, created and con-

---

[1] See Baxter's description of "The English Diocesan Frame of Episcopacy," which, he says, all the Nonconformists were of one mind in regarding as "unlawful, and of dangerous tendency in the Churches." He names as leading objections the great size of the parishes, quite beyond the pastoral control of the clergy, the lack of power to admonish scandalous persons or to judge of men's fitness as communicants, the wholly mechanical and unspiritual procedure of Episcopal Excommunication administered by Lay Chancellors and commonly commuted for a fine. "I have been in most parts of England, and in fifty years' time I never saw one do penance, or confess his sin in public for any scandalous crime : nor ever heard of but two in the Country where I lived (that stood in a white sheet for adultery) except in the space when Bishops were down, and then I have heard of many that have penitently confessed their sin, and begged the prayers of the congregation, and been prayed for" (*v. Autobiography*, i. p. 398).

trolled by the State. The theocratic conception of the Church, which Calvin formed and expressed in his *Institutes*, was intolerant of this subordination of the ecclesiastical to the civil power. In a protracted conflict with the Genevan State he asserted for the Church, and in the end enforced, the claim of independence in the matter of moral and spiritual discipline, and, above all, he created an ecclesiastical machinery for administering such discipline. This machinery was successively adopted by the Reformed Churches of France (1559), of the Netherlands (1568), and of Scotland (1570). In England the medieval courts substantially continued, and, with the formidable addition of the High Commission, administered discipline down to the time when the Long Parliament abolished the whole existing system. An irregular authority over faith and morals was for a while exercised by the Houses of Parliament, but this clearly could not be a permanent arrangement. When Presbyterianism had been accepted, it would seem to follow that its characteristic discipline would be accepted with it; but, as a matter of fact, a determined opposition was made at this point, and, in the sequel, a compromise was effected. The Presbyterian discipline was established, but with limitations and safeguards which secured the ultimate authority of Parliament. On June 9th, 1646, the final Ordinance was agreed upon, and four days later the London ministers were ordered to put the Church government into execution.

(4) *The Jus Divinum of Presbytery.* On this point there was an irreconcilable difference between the Assembly and the Parliament and that secular temper of the English mind which the Parliament represented. The notion that Christ instituted a form of Church government, and bound it as a perpetual ordinance upon the Church, was the common assumption of Papist, Episcopalian, Presbyterian, and Independent; but in the hands of the Presbyterian it became the very keystone of his whole religious system. This was at once its strength and its weakness. "We claim our power of Jesus Christ" was a formula which, spoken undoubtingly in the smallest kirk-sessions, gave to the lay-elders in their own eyes, and in those of their fellow-believers and of their victims, a dignity and a weight which no official of the State could secure for his earth-born authority. But, as clearly, the implied claim was too lofty for real life. It did not admit of the indispensable opportunism of politics. There was in it power neither to learn nor to unlearn. Within the sphere of its own interests no State can really admit the claim of Divine authority anywhere save in itself, and how wide that sphere is can only be determined by ex-

perience. As soon as the claim to a *Jus Divinum* was advanced, the essential Erastianism of Parliament became apparent. "The civil magistrate," said Sir Benjamin Rudyard in the House of Commons, "is a Church officer in every Christian Commonwealth." The issue had not been decided when the whole Presbyterian experiment collapsed. "The Assembly melted away into oblivion, with its claim of the *Jus Divinum* still upon its head dishonoured and unsubstantiated."

(5) *Ordination.* This was a matter of practical urgency. While divines were arguing preachers were dying, and no fresh ones were coming on to fill the vacancies created by death. By a series of Ordinances the Parliament empowered the new-established "Classical Presbyteries" to examine candidates and ordain them. The rules for Ordination required the expectant to have taken the Covenant, and this came to be of no small importance at a later period when many of the clergy ordained under these Parliamentary Ordinances had to determine their attitude towards the Restoration Settlement. The terms of the Covenant were not, at least in England, held to be inconsistent with a restoration of Episcopacy, provided that the restored Episcopacy were not, in the old sense, prelatic and hierarchic; but the actual course of events prevented any real modification, and, when

the Savoy Conference met, the returned Episcopalians knew themselves to be secure. It is not sufficiently remembered that the unhappy pledges which, in the Covenant, the Presbyterian clergy had taken, destroyed much of their liberty of action and made an accommodation with their rivals almost impossible.

(6) *The Directory of Worship.* The Prayer-book—" the great idol of England," as Baillie terms it—had, of course, shared the fate of the hierarchy, and something had to be provided to take its place. There was great repugnance manifested in the Assembly at the Scotch proposal that communicants should be required to come to the Lord's Table to receive the sacrament. The tradition of the English Puritans was to insist on having the consecrated elements brought to them in their seats, and no innovation had been more bitterly resented than Laud's rule as to receiving the sacrament kneeling at an altar rail. Baptism proved to be a hardly less contentious subject than Holy Communion, for there the burning question of dipping *versus* sprinkling came up. On the whole, however, the proceedings were expeditious, and on March 5th, 1645, the whole Directory was adopted by Parliament. The title, as adopted, is this : "*A Directory for the Public Worship of God throughout the three Kingdoms of England, Scotland, and Ireland, together*

with an Ordinance of Parliament for the taking away of the Book of Common Prayer, and for establishing and observing of this present Directory throughout the kingdom of England and dominion of Wales." The new book was forthwith ordered to be used, but to little effect until Parliament attached penalties to the continued use of the Prayer-book.

The *Confession of Faith* (7) and the *Larger and Smaller Catechisms* (8) need not concern us here, for neither had much effect in England. "It is not a little curious," justly observes Mr. Shaw, "that those portions of accomplished work which have remained through later times the most distinct and memorable accomplishment of the Assembly—*i.e.* the Confession of Faith and the Larger Catechism —should have never received the assent of the Parliament which had called the Assembly into being, and at whose behest it had prepared those works."[1]

The Westminster Assembly was also charged with the revision of the metrical version of the Psalms (9), and accordingly revised and recommended to Parliament the version made by Francis Rous, Provost of Eton. This revised version was "authorised by Parliament for general use, and adopted by the committee of estates in Scotland, where it still retains its popularity."[2]

---

[1] Shaw, vol. i. p. 376.   [2] *Dict. of N. B.*, vol. xlix. p. 317.

It is one thing to draft an ecclesiastical system and to enact its establishment, it is quite another thing actually to establish it. The former had, not without friction and delay, been the achievement of the Westminster Assembly, and its author and rather despotic master the Long Parliament. What about the latter? How far was the Presbyterian polity set up in the country? How far was the Prayer-book displaced by the Directory of Worship, discipline enforced by the *lay-elders*, and ordinations administered by the *classes*? Broadly it may be said that the Presbyterian experiment was never seriously attempted over the greater part of the country. Only in London and Lancashire was the parliamentary scheme officially adopted, and even there, almost immediately, it reached a deadlock over the thorny question of discipline. The scheme assumed throughout the friendly co-operation of the civil power, and, after the triumph of the army, that co-operation was refused. The "*classes*" almost everywhere sank into "examining and ordaining bodies, and their records consist of little more than the account of the various examinations and ordinations of candidates." "In their disappointment at the non-success of their Church system the Presbyterian clergy almost in a body made up their minds not to administer the sacrament at all where they could not administer it in the way they wished. Their system required that the sacrament should be guarded from the ignorant and scandalous by means of the eldership. Parishioners proposing to communicate were to submit themselves to instruction by catechising, and to examination by the eldership, and only such as could pass the ordeal were to be accounted fit to receive."[1] But against this system, necessarily inquisitorial and running counter to English habits of thought and life, the dislike of the people presented a sullen resistance, which the ministers were unable to overcome. The parishes refused to elect *lay-elders*, and quietly ignored the admonitions, rebukes, and menaces of the *classes*. Without the assistance of the State there was no means of coercing the parishioners to elect, and without election there was no means of " fencing the tables " by discipline. Zealous ministers made their acceptance of parochial charge conditional on the election of lay-elders. The parishioners preferred to have no ministers at all. It is stated in a petition of the Provincial Synod of London to the Lord Mayor and Common Council in 1648 that no less than forty parish churches were vacant within the Province.[2]

The collapse of the State system occasioned the

---

[1] *v*. Shaw, vol. ii. p. 142.
[2] The list is given in Shaw, vol. ii. p. 103, note.

organisation of voluntary associations to secure such a measure of discipline as would enable conscientious ministers to administer the Sacraments. Of these associations the most famous was that founded by RICHARD BAXTER in Worcester, and described in his *Autobiography*, and more generally in the Preface to his famous treatise on pastoral work, *Gildas Salvianus; or, the Reformed Pastor*. Reason and charity gained at the expense of Presbyterian orthodoxy. Baxter explains the origin of his attempt in the urgent need of his people. "The state of my own congregation, and the necessity of my duty, constrained me to make some attempt. For I must administer the Sacraments to the Church, and the ordinary way of examining every man before they come, I was not able to prove necessary, and the people were averse to it: so that I was forced to think of the matter more seriously: and having determined of that way which was, I thought, most agreeable to the Word of God, I thought, if all the ministers did accord together in one way, the people would much more easily submit, than to the way of any minister that was singular. To attempt their consent I had two very great encouragements: the one was an honest, humble, tractable people at home, engaged in no party, *Prelatical*, Presbyterian, or Independent, and not past four or five of them *Episcopal*, but loving godliness and peace, and hating schism as that which they perceived to tend to the ruin of religion. The other was a company of honest, godly, serious, humble ministers in the country where I lived, *who were not one of them, that associated, Presbyterian or Independent, and not past four or five of them Episcopal, but disengaged faithful men*. At a lecture at Worcester I first procured a meeting, and told them of the design, which they all approved : they imposed it upon me to draw up a form of agreement. The matter of it was to consist, 'So much of the Church Order and Discipline, as the Episcopal, Presbyterian, and Independent are agreed in, as belonging to the pastors of each particular church. . . .'

"According to their desire, I drew up some Articles for our consent, which might engage us to the most effectual practice of so much discipline as might reduce the churches to order, and satisfy ministers in administering the sacraments, and stop the more religious people from separation, to which the unreformedness of the churches through want of discipline inclined them, and yet might not at all contradict the judgments of any of the three parties; and I brought in the reasons of the several points, which, after sufficient examination and deliberation (with the alteration of some few words), were consented to by all the ministers that were present. And after several meetings we subscribed them, and so associated for our mutual help and concord in our work. The ministers that thus associated were for number, parts, and piety, the most considerable part of all that county, and some out of some neighbouring counties that were near us. *There was, not that I know of, one thorough Presbyterian among them, because there was but one such that I knew of in all the county*, and he lived somewhat remote. . . .

"Having all agreed in this association, we proposed publicly to our people so much as required their consent and practice, and gave every family a copy in print, and a sufficient time to consider and understand it, and then put it into execution. . . .

"In our association we agreed upon a monthly meeting at certain market towns for conference about such cases of discipline as required consultation and consent. Accordingly at Evesham and Kidderminster they were constantly kept up. In the town where I lived we had once a month a meeting of three Justices of the Peace, who lived with us, and three or four ministers, for so many we were in the parish, myself and assistants, and three or four deacons, and *twenty of the ancient and godly men of the congregation, who pretended to no office as Lay-elders*, but only met as the trustees of the whole Church to be present and secure their liberties, and do that which any of the Church might do ; and they were chosen once a year hereunto . . . because all the people could not have leisure to meet so oft to debate things which required their consent. At this meeting we admonished those that remained impenitent in any scandalous sin, after more private admonition before two or three ; and we did with all possible tenderness persuade them to repentance, and labour to convince them of their sin and danger ; and pray with them if they consented. And if they could not be prevailed with to repent, we required them to meet before all the ministers at the other monthly meeting, which was always the next day after this parochial meeting. There we renewed our admonitions and exhortations, and some ministers of other parishes laboured to set it home, that the offender might not think it was only the opinion of the pastor of the place, and that he did it out of ill-will or partiality. If he yielded penitently to confess his sin and promise amendment, more or less publicly according to the nature of the scandal, we then joined in prayer for his true repentance and forgiveness, and exhorted him farther to his duty for the future ; but if he still continued obstinately impenitent, by the consent of all, he was by the pastor of the place to be publicly admonished and prayed for by that Church, usually three several days together ; and if he still remained impenitent the Church was required to avoid him as a person unfit for their communion. . . ."

In this interesting narrative there are several points which merit attention. In the first place, Baxter's indifference to Presbyterianism, as such, is very apparent. He aims at a rational compromise which shall enable men of goodwill to get to work; he has no regard for any ecclesiastical system. In the next place, it is clear that, while Puritanism prevailed in that part of England, Presbyterianism was practically unknown. A few of the clergy were "Episcopal," which, in Baxter's usage, means conformist Puritan, men who desired a reformed Episcopacy of the Ussherian type: none were Presbyterian or Prelatical. Then it is noticeable that Baxter is plainly anxious to protect himself from the not unlikely supposition that his committee of "ancient and godly men of the congregation" were really in fact, though not in name, "lay-elders," his anxiety in this respect indicating the special dislike which that part of the Scotch system provoked in the English mind. The discipline attempted by the voluntary associations was certainly, from the standpoint of Scotch orthodoxy, a halting and ineffectual thing. Baxter describes his work at Kidderminster, and the many circumstances, personal and local, which favoured it.

Astonishing results were obtained—results which only his extraordinary fervour and assiduous labours could have obtained; but it is impossible to miss the sense of failure emerging in the narrative, or to dispute the fact that a few years of Baxter's ministry made the mass of the people ready to welcome back the old, indulgent, indolent Prelatism.

"The congregations were usually full, so that we were fain to build five galleries after my coming thither (the church itself being very capacious, and the most commodious and convenient, that ever I was in). Our private meetings also were full. On the Lord's days there was no disorder to be seen in the streets, but you might hear an hundred families singing psalms and repeating sermons, as you passed through the streets. In a word, when I came thither first, there was about one family in a street that worshipped God and called on His Name, and when I came away there were some streets where there was not past one family in the side of a street that did not so; and that did not by professing serious godliness, give us hopes of their sincerity: and those families which were the worst, being inns and alehouses, usually some persons in each house did seem to be religious. Though our administration of the Lord's Supper was so ordered as displeased many, and the far greater part kept away themselves, yet we had 600 that were communicants, of whom there were not twelve that I had not good hopes of, as to their sincerity: and those few that did consent to our communion, and yet lived scandalously were excommunicated afterward: and I hope there were many that had the fear of God that came not to our communion in the sacrament, some of them being kept off by husbands, by parents, by masters, and some dissuaded by men that differed from us: those many that kept away yet took it patiently, and did not revile us, as doing them wrong, and those unruly young men that were excommunicated, bore it patiently as to their outward behaviour, though their hearts were full of bitterness. . . . When I set upon personal conference with each family and catechizing them, there were very few families in all the town that refused to come: and those few were beggars at the town's end, who were so ignorant that they were ashamed it should be manifest. And few families went from me without tears, or seemingly serious promises for a godly life. Yet many ignorant and ungodly persons there were still among us. . . ."[1]

Kidderminster contained, according to Baxter, no less than 1,600 persons old enough to be communicants. Of these he only claims 600 as actually being admitted to communion: that unreconciled major-

---

[1] *Autobiography*, i. pp. 84, 85.

ity, nearly two-thirds of the people, were chafing against the humiliations imposed on them and the restraints imposed on their liberty by Puritanical magistrates, kept up to the mark by the pastor's fiery zeal; and they showed their feelings when the time came. Baxter stands out from the mass of his contemporaries as a liberal, fair-minded man; in his hands the system would be comparatively moderate and reasonable, but in the hands of lesser men it would become quickly intolerable. Certain it is that both the formal Presbyterianism of London and Lancashire and the quasi-Presbyterianism of the voluntary associations throughout the country fell before the impatience of the people, so soon as the political situation made the revelation of that impatience possible.

Thus, then, the Presbyterian experiment failed almost as soon as it was seriously tried. It is an interesting question why this should have happened. The passionate enthusiasm with which the destruction of the episcopal government was pressed forward in the early stages of the Long Parliament proved the strength of the resentment provoked by the Laudian administration, and facilitated the establishment of that Presbyterian polity, which, as matters then stood, was the only possible alternative to Episcopacy; but it implied no genuine popular sentiment in favour of the new system, which, for many reasons, was little likely to commend itself to the acceptance of Englishmen. In the first place, Presbyterianism was a foreign system, and then, as now, whatever was foreign was, to that extent, suspicious in English eyes. In the next place, Presbyterianism, though in form oligarchic, is, in spirit, essentially democratic. It suited the republican tradition of Switzerland and Holland, and, in Scotland itself, was repudiated after an interval by the greater part of the nobility and gentry. The English genius is not democratic. When Charles II. said that Presbyterianism was no religion for a gentleman, he spoke the mind of the nation. But, these disadvantages apart, the failure of Presbyterianism was inevitable so soon as the attempt was made seriously to apply that discipline, which was its most distinctive, and not least honourable, characteristic. Aristocratic in social sentiment, intensely conservative in his habit of thought, the Englishman, within the sphere of his own personal and domestic life, is the most jealously independent of all men. His home is his castle, his religion is his own secret, and his morals his own affair. Let but the attempt be made to push authority into that sphere, to examine his orthodoxy and regulate his behaviour, and he will manifest at once an attitude of relentless and unreasoning hostility. This desperate attempt the Presbyterian system required, and, therefore, that system was repudiated with a promptitude and decision which have no parallel elsewhere. The accusation of pride levelled at Presbyterianism is suggestive. There was clearly a plausibility in the accusation which arrested attention. Butler, in his coarse satire, gives expression to a widely felt sentiment. Pride is the prevailing element in his description of Presbyterianism.

> "Great piety consists in Pride;
> To rule is to be sanctify'd:
> To domineer, and to controul,
> Both o'er the body and the soul,
> Is the most perfect discipline
> Of Church Rule, and by Right Divine.
>
> . . . . .
>
> Presbytery does but translate
> The Papacy to a free state.
> A Common-wealth of Popery,
> Where every village is a See
> As well as Rome, and must maintain
> A Tythe-Pig Metropolitan."[1]

The origin of this unamiable quality must be sought rather in the Calvinistic doctrine than in the Presbyterian polity. The belief in divine election of the few and divine predestination to ruin of the many can hardly fail to breed arrogance in the chosen few. Spiritual privilege is perhaps the most demoralising form of privilege. The history of

---

[1] *v. Hudibras*, part i., canto iii., 1175-1180, 1201-1206.

religion seems to make it evident that a rigid dogma readily commends itself to the acceptance of men of a low moral type. Antinomianism is the historic parasite of spiritual privilege, and the Presbyterian Calvinists illustrated the general law. Moreover, Presbyterianism was bound to the Calvinistic theology just at the moment when that theology was losing its hold on human intelligence. This fact became aggressively prominent when the question of religious toleration was raised by the Independents. The Presbyterian system, as it was conceived and defended in the seventeenth century, was as hostile to the notion of toleration as the medieval Papacy. Men found the most vehement obstacle to religious liberty in the very system which seemed daily in itself less tolerable. Presbyterianism, in short, united the attributes of obsoleteness and arrogance. Therefore it raised against itself the most formidable array of opponents conceivable. Men of tender conscience and of no conscience at all, the latitudinarian in belief and the Epicurean in practice, the zealot for liberty, and the Erastian in political theory, in a word, the thoughtful, the tolerant, the sensitive, and the worldly, combined to overthrow, trample upon, and revile a system which had succeeded in wounding and exasperating them all. And yet he must be a careless or prejudiced student of the later history of the English Church who would infer from the failure of the Presbyterian experiment in the seventeenth century a conclusion unfavourable to the character of the Puritanism which for the time ruled and failed with it. If there be any truth in the statement that the English Church, in spite of many faults, has sustained in the nation with unequalled success the notion that religion is essentially moral and can never tolerate the severance of devotion and right conduct, the fact is in great part due to the Puritan protest against a mundane Church and the low standard of religious habit which it permitted and fostered. If the English clergy have maintained a higher conception of pastoral duty than has prevailed elsewhere, the fact is, to a great extent, the result of Puritan theory and practice during the anarchic period of a nominal Presbyterian supremacy. The latitudinarian divines of the Revolution epoch are the true spiritual children of the Puritan Presbyterians of the previous generation. It is sufficiently suggestive that the Puritan Baxter has left behind him not only the most striking example of pastoral activity which that age can produce, but also the most moving and valuable treatise of pastoral duty which our religious literature contains. The moral of the story is the futility of the attempt to ignore terrestrial conditions of spiritual movements.

Puritanism was home-born, redolent of the English soil, akin to the English character; Presbyterianism was alien, and distasteful to Englishmen. The association of the two was arbitrary, shortlived, and injurious. Puritanism was hampered and discredited by the polity to which "by the fatal surrender of 1643 to Scotch Presbytery" it found itself bound; Presbyterianism never had a fair chance in England. Across the Border it gained and held the ardent attachment of a strong, proud nation, which was the better for its stern discipline, and found in its simple forms the sufficient expressions of its piety. Here it was an exotic and a parasite. The Nonconformist Churches are the progeny of Puritanism; they owe nothing but unhelpful political memories to the Presbyterian experiment.

Erastianism

1524. Birth of Thomas Erastus.
1568. Erastus writes *Theses*.
1583. Death of Erastus.
1589. Publication of the *Theses* and *Confirmatio Thesium*.
1594. Publication of Hooker's *Ecclesiastical Polity*, Books I.–IV.
1597. Publication of *Ecclesiastical Polity*, Book V.
1603. Bancroft's Canons.
1640. Laud's Canons.
1643–6. The Erastians in the Westminster Assembly and Parliament oppose the *jus divinum* of Presbytery.
1648. Publication of Hooker's *Ecclesiastical Polity*, Books VI. and VIII.
1651. Publication of Hobbes' *Leviathan*.
1654. Death of Selden.
1659. English Translation of *Theses* of Erastus.
1662. Publication of Hooker's *Ecclesiastical Polity*, Book VII.
1673. The Test Act.

I

ERASTIANISM stands in common usage for so many different, and not always very obviously connected opinions that it may, perhaps, be useful to take pains to show what it properly is, and how it came to mean so much.

Thomas Erastus was born in Baden in Switzerland in 1524 of humble parents. At the age of sixteen he moved to Basel, where he pursued his studies, and was fortunate enough to find a patron, by whose assistance he was enabled to continue at the university. After visiting Italy and studying philosophy at Bologna, he returned to Germany and practised medicine at the court of the Prince of Henneberg. Thence he was invited by Frederick III., Prince Elector Palatine, to fill the professorship of physics in the University of Heidelberg, and to act as principal court physician. Heidelberg was just then the scene of embittered controversy, for the Elector was forcing into acceptance the "Reformed," that is the Calvinist, system of faith and discipline in place of the Lutheranism, which had formerly obtained. The introduction in 1562 of a catechism, in which the Calvinist view of the Lord's Supper is set forth, led to a lively conflict, in which Brenz in Stuttgart, on the Lutheran side, attacked, and Bullinger and Beza, the champions of Calvinism, defended it. To bring the dissension to an end the Elector arranged a conference at Maulbronn in 1564, at which Erastus was commanded to assist, and which, so far from composing, further aggravated the religious disputes. Six years later the Elector ordered the introduction of presbyteries, and Erastus, accused of sympathy with the Socinians, was excommunicated by the new authority. In

1575 the sentence was reconsidered and reversed, but his position at Heidelberg was no longer easy. In 1580 he retired to Basel, where he died three years later, and was buried in St. Martin's Church. On his tomb was placed a laudatory inscription, in which he is described as "an acute philosopher, a skilled physician, a sincere theologian." He is said to have been a man of blameless life, and singular zeal for the truth, ready at all times to acknowledge error, but sceptical of unsifted statements.

"Neither had he any man's authority in such esteem, that it could move him to depart from what was evident to sense, or agreeable to reason; but he always judged that truth was to be taken from the matter itself, and not from authority."[1]

"As an investigator of nature he was honourably distinguished by his adherence to a sound inductive method. Most of the works that appeared during his lifetime were directed against the fantastic notions of Paracelsus and his school,"[2] but he fails to rise above the superstition of his age when, in his treatise on the subject, he urges that witches should be put to death.

The ecclesiastical writings, which have made the name of Erastus immortal, were never published during his lifetime. They consist of two works,

---

[1] Dr. Lee's *Theses of Erastus*, Preface, p. xii.
[2] *Encyclopædia Britannica*, vol. viii. p. 518.

bound up in a single, rather slender quarto, bearing the date 1589. The two works are the *Theses* and the *Confirmatio Thesium*, the latter directed against Beza and the other opponents of the *Theses*. "The indignation which the opinions maintained in them had occasioned seems to have rendered the publication dangerous, as both the printer's name and the place are suppressed on the title-page of the original edition and fictitious names substituted.[1] The work was reprinted at Amsterdam A.D. 1649, and an English translation of the Theses appeared in London the year before the Restoration."[2]

---

[1] *v.* Selden, De Synedriis, c. x. [*Works*, vol. i. tom. 2, pp. 1019–21], says that the book was published in London by John Wolfe, with the approval of Archbishop Whitgift, and at the instance of other leading English ecclesiastics.

"Ab Erasti vidua, aut a Castelvetro, cui nupta illa est, autographum impetrarant viri aliquot ex ordine ecclesiastico in Anglia summi, qui etiam in regimine publico partes tunc agebant hic primarias. Atque eorum auspiciis jussuque typis et mandatum. Placuit quidem illis ut non sine fictorum loci et typographi nominum larva prodiret; quale pro hominum arbitrio saepius fit."

Selden says that he had seen in the Lambeth Library, lately removed to Cambridge, a volume of Erastus's *Theses*, which he believed to be the printer's presentation copy to Archbishop Whitgift.

[2] Lee, p. xvii., xviii. The title of the book is the following: "Explicatio gravissimae Quaestionis utrum Excommunicatio, quatenus Religionem intelligentes et amplexantes, a Sacramentorum usu, propter admissum facinus arcet, mandato nitatur divino an excogitata sit ab hominibus."

In an interesting preface addressed to "the pious and truth-regarding Reader," Erastus explains how he came to write the *Theses*.

"It is about sixteen years ago (*i.e.* 1568) since some men were seized on by a certain excommunicatory fever, which they did adorn with the title of ecclesiastical discipline, and did contend that it was holy and commanded of God to the Church: and which they earnestly did desire should be imposed on the whole Church. They affirmed the manner thereof to be this: that some certain presbyters should sit in the name of the whole Church, and should judge who were worthy or unworthy to come unto the Lord's Supper." Alarmed at this project, Erastus first protested against it on practical grounds as unsuitable in a community in which "scarcely the thirtieth part of the people did understand or approve the Reformed religion," and then proceeded to examine it with the aid of all the authorities he could discover—schoolmen, modern writers, finally the scriptures.

"After this I did confer about my thoughts with good, holy, and learned men, and I did exhort them that they should not lightly ponder the cause. For it seemed to me most unnecessary to put two heads upon one body of a visible Church, whose commands, decrees, and government were already diverse, so that the rule of the one was not subject to the care of the other, but the government of each in its own kind was supreme. Indeed they would have had their ecclesiastical senate or presbytery so constitute, that it should have the supreme power of punishing of vices, yea, in the magistrates themselves : notwithstanding, not with corporal punishments, but with the debarring them from the sacrament, first privately, and if this did not succeed well, then next solemnly and publicly. But I said, I did believe that one magistrate, appointed by God, could as well now bridle all transgressors as he could of old." Erastus confined himself to private discussions, fearing to cause disturbance in the church, but at last his hand was forced. It is not uninteresting that the occasion of public conflict was one of our own countrymen, carrying abroad, then, as Englishmen have so often done since, the domestic religious bickerings of Britain. "It fell out afterwards that an Englishman,[1] who was said to have left his country by reason of certain vestures in the church, desired to be graduate doctor, and did propose a dispute concerning indifferent things and vestures. This dispute our theologues would

---

[1] Selden names him. "Occasionem autem proximam unde, ut videtur, ortae sunt theses illae nactus est Erastus ex disputatione Heidelbergae habita, praeside D. Petro Boquino, respondente pro gradu doctorali *M. Georgio Withero Anglo*, anno 1568, 10 junii, in qua de disciplina hac seu excommunicatione controvertebatur" (*l.c.*, p. 1017).

not admit, lest they should offend the English . . . wherefore amongst other theses he proposed this, that it behoved in each right constitute Church this order should be kept, that the ministers, with their presbytery chosen for that purpose, should have power to excommunicate any sinners, yea, princes themselves."

This disputation of the Englishman was as the letting out of the water, and together with the rest Erastus was swept along by the tide of controversy. He had a natural fondness for intellectual conflict. "He did wonderfully extol school disputes," observes his biographer, "in respect they did exercise both invention and judgment, and confirm the same. And further, he constantly professed that he never returned from any of those disputes, but always bettered." Being busy just then with a batch of invalided soldiers, he "noted down his thoughts in pieces as they occurred to him," and showed his notes to others with a request for their opinion on them. Finally he "contracted" them into a set of theses, which were widely circulated in manuscript throughout Germany. On his death-bed he ordered his theses to be published.[1]

---

[1] So the title-page of the *Theses* states: "Opus nunc recens ex ipsius Autoris authographo erutum, et in lucem, *prout moriens jusserat*, editum."

II

The question with which Erastus is concerned is stated in the IXth thesis: "Whether any person ought, because of his having committed a sin, or of his living an impure life, to be prohibited from the use and participation of the sacraments with his fellow-Christians, provided he wishes to partake with them? ..." "Whether any command or any example can be produced from the Holy Scriptures, requiring or intimating that such persons should be excluded from the sacraments?" He then reviews the evidence of the Bible, examining with much acuteness the passages advanced in defence of excommunication. In the XXIIIrd thesis he sums up his conclusions as to the Old Testament. "This, then, remains firm and immovable that, in the Old Testament, none was debarred from the sacraments on account of the immorality of his conduct: but, on the contrary, the pious priests, prophets, judges, kings, and finally that most illustrious and holy forerunner of our Lord, John the Baptist, instead of debarring, rather invited all the people to the celebration of the sacrament, as the law required them to do." The substantial identity of the Jewish and the Christian sacraments being asserted on the authority of St. Paul, the inference from the practice disclosed in the Old Testament is manifest, and stated in the XXVth thesis. "For, as we properly urge against the Anabaptists this very valid argument, that, because baptism has come in the place of circumcision, and Christ nowhere forbade the baptizing of infants, therefore we are no less permitted to baptize our infants than the Jews to circumcise theirs. So, in the case before us, we may reason no less conclusively in this manner. The Lord's Supper has come in the room of the Passover. But men's sins were not punished by denying them the Passover, nor was any one kept back from it on account of his sins; but, on the contrary, all the people, especially males, were, by the Law of Moses, invited to join in the celebration of it. And seeing we nowhere read that this principle has been superseded, or abolished, therefore the people's sins are not to be punished *now* by refusing them the Lord's Supper, neither is any one for that reason to be kept back." Erastus then examines the evidence of the New Testament, and with great skill turns the sacramental theory of his Calvinistic opponents to the service of his argument. "Do not almost all divines hold the sacraments to be visible words, and to exhibit to the eyes what words express to the ear? Why, then, do we go about to exclude nobody from the word, while from the sacraments, especially the Lord's Supper, we would exclude some, and that contrary to, or at least without, the express command of God? Because, say they, the word was appointed for all men, the sacraments only for those who are converted. I know it: and I am not speaking of admitting Mohammedans or unconverted pagans, but those who are called by God into His church, and engrafted into it, who approve of its doctrines, and who appear at least desirous to use the sacraments properly" [XXXVIII.]. His examination of his opponent's case leads him in the LXVIIIth thesis to "the correct and true conclusion, that this excommunication, by which Christians are debarred solely on account of unholiness of life from the sacraments, is not an ordinance of God, but an invention and a device of men; and, so far from having any foundation in the sacred scriptures, these can be shown rather to prohibit it." "I see no reason," he continues in thesis LXXIII., "why the Christian magistrate at the present day should not possess the same power which God commanded the magistrate to exercise in the Jewish commonwealth. . . ." "Wherefore" (thesis LXXIV.), "if that Church and State were most wisely founded, arranged, and appointed, any other must merit approbation which approaches to its form as nearly as present times and circumstances will permit. So that wherever the magistrate is godly and Christian, there is no need of any other authority, under any other pretension or title, to rule or punish the people—as if the Christian magistrate differed nothing from the heathen. 'Of all errors in truth,' says Wolfgang Musculus, in his *Common Places, De Magistratu*, from which book the words immediately preceding are quoted, 'of all errors, in truth, the most hurtful is this, which a great many people entertain, that the Christian magistrate is to be viewed in the same light in which we regard a heathen government, whose authority is to be recognised only in respect of secular matters.' If, then, the Christian magistrate possesses not only the authority to settle religion according to the directions given in holy scripture, and to arrange the ministries and offices thereof —for which reason Moses requires him who should be elected king to transcribe with his own hand the Book of the Law, or writings of Moses, and to exercise himself in the study of these continually—but also, in like manner, to punish crimes: in vain do some among us now meditate the setting up a new kind of tribunal, which would bring down the magistrate himself to the rank of a subject of other men. I allow, indeed, the magistrate ought to consult, where *doctrine* is concerned, those who have particularly studied it; but that there should be any such ecclesiastical tribunal to take cognizance of men's conduct, we find no such thing anywhere appointed in the holy scriptures." The concluding thesis deals with the case of churches "under an ungodly government (for example, Popish, or Mohammedan)." He holds that voluntary officers should be appointed to act as arbitrators, and to unite with the ministers in maintaining moral discipline by admonition, reproof, refusal of private intercourse, and public rebuke. "But from the sacrament which God has instituted, they may not debar any who desire to partake. For who but God is the judge of men's hearts? It may happen that some spark may be kindled by the public preaching, which it may be not at all useless, but rather most beneficial, to cherish by every means not inconsistent with piety. And tell me, I pray, how it can be otherwise than absurd, and therefore impious, to debar from a solemn thanksgiving and commemoration of the death of the Lord, a person who declares that he feels his heart prompts him so to do?—that he desires with the Church to celebrate that death, and to be a member of the Church, and, finally, that he wishes to testify that he disapproves his past life."

III

The *Theses* of Erastus were published in 1589, five years later appeared the first four books of Hooker's *Ecclesiastical Polity*. In his preface Hooker refers to the circumstances which occasioned the writing of the *Theses*, and the "controversy which sprang up between Beza and Erastus about the matter of excommunication," in consequence. His judgment was not wholly favourable to either combatant. "In which disputation," he says, "they have, as to me it seemeth, divided very equally the truth between them: Beza most truly maintaining the necessity of excommunication, Erastus as truly the non-necessity of lay-elders to be ministers thereof."[1] It is well known that the last three books of Hooker's great work were published long after his death, and under circumstances which justly arouse suspicion as to their authenticity. The sixth and eighth books appeared together in 1648, the seventh in Bishop Gauden's edition in 1662. On the literary question we may well accept Mr. Sidney Lee's conclusion that "the seventh and eighth books, in their existing shape, are constructed from Hooker's rough notes, and, although imperfect, are

---

[1] *Works*, vol. i. p. 175 (Keble's Edition).

pertinent to his scheme : but that the so-called sixth book has no right to its place in Hooker's treatise."[1] It is with the eighth book only that we are here concerned. It may be taken as a representative statement of Anglican doctrine on the subject of the relations of Church and State. In common with Erastus, and, indeed, with all his contemporaries, Hooker assumes, and makes the basis of argument, that analogy between the Jewish monarchy and church and the Christian, which lies at the bottom of so much mental confusion, and gives to the writings of that age an aspect so grotesque and arbitrary. This analogy implies the further assumption that, as in ancient Israel, the extent of Church and nation is absolutely identical. "In a word, our estate is according to the pattern of God's own ancient elect people, which people was not part of them the commonwealth, and part of them the Church of God, but the self-same people whole and entire were both under one chief Governor, on whose supreme authority they did all depend."[2] The Royal Supremacy is determined as to its character and extent by the testimony of the Old Testament. As the Jewish monarch was subject to the law of Moses, so is the Christian monarch bound to the gospel. "For the received

---

[1] *Dict. of Nat. Biog.*, vol xxvii. p. 293.
[2] *Works*, vol. iii. part i. p. 425.

laws of liberty of the Church the king hath supreme authority and power, but against them none."[1] Hooker repudiates with some scorn the notion that the king's business can be properly limited to the material concerns of the commonwealth. "A gross error it is, to think that regal power ought to serve for the good of the body, and not of the soul; for men's temporal peace, and not for their eternal safety: as if God had ordained kings for no other end and purpose but only to fat up men like hogs, and to see that they have their mast."[2] Descending to particulars, Hooker examines in detail the actual authority possessed by the monarch over the national Church. He defends the much-criticised title "Head of the Church," as being nothing more than a convenient statement of the fact. "If the having of supreme power be allowed, why is the expressing thereof by the title of head condemned?"[3] It is curious that he seems unconscious of the fact, which had not been without significance at the time, that the title "Supreme Head" had not been revived with the supremacy which it expressed, when Elizabeth re-established the system of Henry VIII. He considers the calling of ecclesiastical assemblies and the making laws about religion. The Apostolic Council of Jerusalem is not to be made a precedent,

---

[1] *Ibid.*, p. 447. [2] *Ibid.*, p. 453. [3] *Ibid.*, p. 460.

as its composition and conditions of meeting were extraordinary. "As now the state of the Church doth stand, kings being not then that which now they are, and the clergy not now that which then they were: till it be proved that some special law of Christ hath for ever annexed unto the clergy alone the power to make ecclesiastical laws, we are to hold it a thing most consonant with equity and reason, that no ecclesiastical laws be made in a Christian commonwealth, without consent of the laity as of the clergy, but least of all without consent of the highest power."[1] To the papist objection that Parliament has no more right "to give order to the Church and clergy" in religious matters than "to make laws for the hierarchies of angels in heaven," Hooker replies with a dignified description of the Parliament, as the organ of the national will, and retorts on his opponent the parliamentary proceedings under Queen Mary when the Houses voted submission to the Pope. "Had they power to repeal laws made, and none to make laws concerning the regiment of the Church?"[2] He justifies the English practice of conjoining the action of the clergy in Convocation with that of the nation in Parliament, by pointing out that, while reason and piety suggest the propriety of taking the matter of laws from the

---

[1] *Ibid.*, p. 505.   [2] *Ibid.*, p. 511.

judgment of the wisest in those things which they are to concern, *i.e.* the pastors and bishops of our souls, yet "it is the general consent of all that giveth them the form and vigour of laws, without which they could be no more unto us than the counsels of physicians to the sick,"[1] and to give such general consent is the sole and incommunicable attribute of Parliament. Hooker goes on to justify the royal power of appointing the bishops as properly consequent on the royal endowment of the bishoprics, and the character of the bishops as spiritual peers. After justifying the king's appellant jurisdiction over the ecclesiastical courts, Hooker brings his treatise to a close by discussing the much debated question of excommunication. Is the king exempt from spiritual censures? His conclusion is that, while the sovereign cannot rightly be subjected to public examination and punishment such as the presbyterian discipline provided, yet he ought to submit himself to such "excommunication as is only a dutiful, religious, and holy refusal to admit notorious transgressors in so extreme degree unto the blessed communion of saints, especially the mysteries of the Body and Blood of Christ, till their humbled penitent minds be made manifest."

"Sith the kings of England are within their own

---

[1] *Ibid.*, p. 513.

dominions the most high, and can have no peer, how is it possible that any, either civil or ecclesiastical, person under them should have over them coercive power, when such power would make that person so far forth his superior's superior, ruler, and judge?"[1] Excommunication "according to the platform of reformed discipline" is declared to be incompatable with the king's "sovereign regiment."

IV

Hooker's doctrine was officially adopted in the *Canons* of 1603, which still are held by the lawyers to have a shadowy and undefined authority over the English clergy. The first canon requires the clergy "four times every year at least, in their sermons and other collations and lectures," to teach that within his dominions the king's power "is the highest power under God": and the second canon binds on the Church that false and unfortunate parallel with ancient Israel, which, as we have seen, confused both Erastus and Hooker. "Whosoever shall hereafter affirm, that the King's Majesty hath not the same authority in causes ecclesiastical, that the godly kings had amongst the Jews and Christian emperors of the primitive Church . . . let

[1] *Ibid.*, p. 569.

him be excommunicated ipso facto." Two circumstances tended to develop Hooker's theory in a very unfortunate direction. The personal character and predilections of the first two Stuarts were eminently favourable to the growth of what may be called Byzantinism. James I., both as a despot in temper and a theological student in habit, was naturally disposed to take literally the current Anglican language about the monarchy. Charles I. made up by strength of conviction and obstinacy of purpose for his inferiority to his father in learning and caution. It was inevitable that in the hands of these sovereigns the royal supremacy should become less legal and constitutional, and more religious and personal. This tendency on the side of the kings coexisted with a kindred tendency on the side of the churchmen. The puritan movement was hostile to kingly independence and to episcopal supremacy alike. "No king, no bishop" expressed a view of the situation which seemed as reasonable to Archbishop Bancroft as to King James. And, therefore, as the episcopal party in the English Church pushed itself into greater prominence, secured the principal patronage, and manipulated in its own interest the machinery of ecclesiastical government, so the sacred character of the kingship was emphasised, and the royal supremacy made to appear a personal attribute of a Christian sovereign, the anointed of the Lord, His vicar and oracle. Hooker, with the philosophic depth and robust common sense which marked his whole treatment of ecclesiastical politics, had perceived and made prominent the representative and constitutional aspects of the kingly office. He had dwelt on the sole power of Parliament to give validity of law to the decisions of the Church : he had made it clear that royal supremacy really meant the supremacy of that law which uttered the general consent of the nation itself. The Jacobean and Caroline ecclesiastics, who served themselves of Hooker's great and justly honoured reputation, were men of another spirit. They separated the King from the Parliament : set prerogative before the general assent : preferred a mysterious divine right vested in a person, to a constitutional authority uttered, secured, controlled by the law. There is a long step from Hooker to Laud, from the grave and balanced reasoning of the *Ecclesiastical Polity* to the astonishing homiletics of the canons of 1640. The words of those canons might be justified by Hooker's argument, but their whole spirit and effect are different. There is something grotesque, at once grimly humorous and oddly pathetic, about those canons of 1640, which summed up the Laudian venture in a declaration of ecclesiastical theory, and which figured so largely in the indictment which the Parliament was about to frame and press relentlessly against the archbishop and his system. The canons begin by renewing with more precision the rule of 1603, which required the clergy four times in the year to exalt the royal supremacy, and then prescribe a lengthy "explanation of the regal power," which they must "treatably and audibly read" to their congregations once a quarter at morning prayer. It is a very characteristic document, exaggerated and at the same time apologetic, the work of a small mind aflame with an immense conviction, yet dimly conscious that there were objections to be answered and risks to be run. The most noticeable feature of the canons is their total silence as to Parliament or the law. The Church is throughout connected solely, as to its supreme control, with the monarch, and there is no suggestion anywhere that the monarch's power is limited by anything save his own sense of duty. The Erastian doctrine is explicitly asserted both against the Papists and the Presbyterians. "For any person or persons to set up, maintain, or avow in any their [*sc.* the king's] said realms or territories respectively, under any pretence whatsoever, any independent coactive power, either papal or popular (whether directly or indirectly), is to undermine their great royal office, and cunningly to overthrow that most sacred ordinance, which God Himself hath established: and so is treasonable against God, as well as against the King." With an obvious reference to the Scotch revolt, it is declared that "for subjects to bear arms against their kings, offensive or defensive, upon any pretence whatsoever" is, in S. Paul's words, "to receive to themselves damnation." Then the burning question of the taxes is dealt with in a curiously feeble paragraph, which begins with an assertion of the King's divine right to receive from his subjects "all manner of necessary support and supply," then, with evident allusion to current controversies, affirms that "nevertheless, subjects have not only possession of, but a true and just right, title, and propriety to, and in all their goods and estates, and ought to have," and concludes with the statement, sufficiently futile at a moment when the country was seething with indignation on the very count of unjust exactions, that "these two are so far from crossing one another, that they mutually go together for the honourable and comfortable support of both. For as it is the duty of the subjects to supply their King, so it is part of the kingly office to support his subjects in the property and freedom of their estates." No allusion to Parliament, no reference to the law, no consciousness of the Constitution! Contrast the language of Hooker: "I am not of opinion that simply always in kings the most, but the best limited power is best; the most limited is, that which may deal in fewest things; the best, that which in dealing is tied unto the soundest, perfectest, and most indifferent rule: which rule is the law: I mean not only the law of nature and of God, but very [? every] national or municipal law consonant thereunto. Happier that people whose law is their king in the greatest things, than that whose king is himself their law. Where the king doth guide the state, and the law the king, that commonwealth is like a harp or melodious instrument, the strings whereof are tuned and handled all by one, following as laws the rules and canons of musical science. . . . The axioms of our regal government are these, '*Lex facit regem*': the king's grant of any favour made contrary to the law is void: '*Rex nihil potest nisi quod jure potest.*'"[1] The second canon laments the negligence of the people in observing with suitable thanksgiving the day of the king's "most happy inauguration," and orders the presentment and punishment of absentees from the parish churches on that day.

Next follow lengthy canons against the growth of Popery, Socinianism, and sectaries (among whom the whole mass of Puritans are, though unnamed, yet unmistakably included, being probably the most part of the religious folk in the kingdom), and then comes the canon which imposed the famous

---

[1] *Works*, vol. iii. part i. pp. 439-40.

"etcetera oath," which may be called the "last straw" of Laudianism on the patience of the English people. The measure of the resentment which it provoked will only be appreciated when it is remembered, that it specifically prohibited that distinction between episcopacy and prelacy, which was the practically universal assumption of English churchmen, apart from the straitest sect of Laudians. Conceive the folly which could propose to a nation, throbbing with religious discontent, a pledge to be taken by all its religious teachers, in whatever capacity, that "they would never consent to alter the government of the Church by archbishops, bishops, deans, and archdeacons, etc., as it stood then established," and to do this, apart from Parliament altogether (though it plainly trenched on the legal and constitutional functions of Parliament), by the king's "prerogative royal and supreme authority in causes ecclesiastical."

The true development of Hooker's theory was towards such a supremacy of Parliament over the Church as did ultimately obtain: but that theory lent itself easily to the misunderstanding of men, preoccupied with an ecclesiastical ideal which seemed for the nonce compatible with the royal supremacy, but was not only intrinsically unreasonable, but could in no way be reconciled with the necessary predominance of Parliament.

V

So long as king and hierarchy were of one mind Laud's Byzantinism was practicable, but he did not contemplate the contingency which had to be faced before the century was out. A vicious king like Charles II. is painful to contemplate and humiliating to obey, but profligacy has never been found incompatible with orthodoxy, and one can always fall back on the distinction between the man and the monarch, but when the king combined popery with profligacy, as James II. actually did, the Laudian scheme became manifestly unworkable. It is one of the ironies of history that the expulsion of the king was the work of men who had spent their lives in preaching the Laudian doctrine of non-resistance. For a brief space the English bishops were popular favourites, but, significantly enough, it was the brief space in which they swallowed their most vaunted principles, and went back on their most venerated precedents. At the time when the Laudian system collapsed, this demonstration of its intrinsic unreasonableness was yet in the distance. Parliament, as we have shown above, adopted Presbyterianism in a panic as a weapon against the king, and only gradually discovered the gravity of its decision, and, as the discovery was made, that decision became increasingly unpalatable. Erastianism was historically a protest against the discipline of Presbyterianism. The point on which Erastus came into conflict with his Calvinist contemporaries was, precisely, the point of excommunication: but that point raised the whole question of the relations of Church and State. Concede the discipline, and, in respect of a large class of human action, you admit an authority within the State greater than the State itself. It must always be remembered that as yet men's minds were governed by the notion that the Church, however organised, must be coextensive with the nation. From that assumption it seemed to follow inevitably, as Hooker argued, that the national institutions alone sufficed for the exercise of ecclesiastical functions. But at this point two classes of difficulty emerged. On the one hand, there is the fact of the Church's spiritual character, which, secured and certified by its divine origin, could never really accept national authority as adequate within the spiritual sphere. The frank recognition of this fact was the strength both of the papist and of the presbyterian: the weakness of both lay in their diverse but kindred misapprehensions of its meaning and practical bearings. On the other hand there is the fact of the individual conscience, which disdains to own an ultimate authority in any institution, whether political or ecclesiastical, and finally confesses the supremacy of its own self. The frank recognition of this fact was the strength of the sectary, now beginning to loom threateningly on the horizon of national politics, but he also misapprehended the bearings of the truth he saw. The royal supremacy was properly Erastian in so far as it secured the single government of Church and State: but the characteristic doctrine of Erastus as to excommunication was adopted by the representatives of no body of religious opinion, and, indeed, implied the negation of a Christian Church conceived as an organised society. The term Erastianism, then, by a legitimate and inevitable extension, came to mean the subordination of the Church to the State in such sense and to such extent, that the effective unity of the commonwealth is secured. The royal supremacy did this, and so long as the monarch, in fact as well as in theory, embodied the national will, the royal supremacy commanded the general acceptance of the nation: under the two first Stuart kings, as has been already explained, the monarchy pursued an ecclesiastical policy of its own, using the constitutional supremacy as a personal prerogative, and, by its means, denationalising the Church. The result was inevitable. The royal supremacy, ceasing to reflect the national will, ceased also to command the national acceptance. At the moment when Presbyterianism crossed the border, and was received at Westminster, it seemed to offer a way of escape from an intolerable ecclesiastical system, which enforced a discipline of its own upon a reluctant people, who resented both its principles and its methods: but hardly had the political crisis passed, and the necessity arisen for seriously considering Presbyterianism as an alternative system, than the old grievance emerged again in a more threatening form. The debates in the Westminster Assembly, and, still more, the debates in Parliament on the *Jus Divinum* of the Presbytery, and the vital question of excommunication revealed a strong, and in the end, prevailing sentiment, which was genuinely Erastian.

VI

The English Erastians were a mixed company. Some were dominated by the undoubted supremacy of the Jewish monarch in religious matters. They claimed for the Christian state an equal authority. Of such men the learned LIGHTFOOT was the most conspicuous representative.[1] Others, notably the

---

[1] *v.* Fuller, *Church History, sub anno* 1644. "Mr. John Coleman, a modest and learned man, beneficed in Lincolnshire, and Mr. John Lightfoot, well skilled in rabbinical learning, were the chief members of the Assembly, who (for the main) maintained

common lawyers, who formed an important, almost a dominating, part of the Long Parliament, were swayed by that dislike and jealousy of the ecclesiastical jurisdiction, which was an immemorial tradition of Westminster Hall, and had been stimulated to the point of conflict by the eager aggressions of Archbishop Laud. "We will have much to do with them," wrote Baillie in April, 1645, "to make sundry of our votes pass, for most of their lawyers are strong Erastians, and would have all the Church government depend absolutely on the Parliament." In close sympathy with the lawyers was a small knot of persons, who superadded the characters of antiquarians and philosophers, and who were represented both in the assembly and in the Parliament by the keen-tongued and erudite SELDEN. They brought to the discussion a knowledge, which for the most part the divines did not possess, and which, even those who did possess it, were eager to ignore, as to the actual course of Christianity in the world. In the pretensions of the Presbyterians, pressed with all the ardour of fresh conviction and accepted in many quarters as new revelations, Selden saw nothing more respectable than a rather shabby

---

the tenets of Erastus. These often produced the Hebrew original for the power of princes in ecclesiastical matters." Coleman's Christian name was not John, but Thomas, and he was known as "Rabbi Coleman."

version of the age-long conflict for secular dominion, which had been waged with the State by ecclesiastics, since ecclesiastics were. He discounted with a sneer the solemn protestations of principle, and dismissed as irrelevant the elaborate arguments from scripture. At bottom the question was practical, and here expediency must be the principle, and precedents the authority. As a matter of fact, whatever the theory, there had never been recognised any such ecclesiastical independence as the Westminster divines were claiming. What the State would not yield to the Papacy, could it be expected to yield to the Presbytery? When a letter from the Zealand churches was read to the House, and a motion was made that it should be read, "Mr. Selden spake earnestly against it, shewing that in that letter they challenged an ecclesiastical or Church government to be *jure divino*, with which the civil magistrate had nothing to do, and this, he said, was contrary to the ancient law of England and the use here received." Selden had his own private reason for distrusting the moral competence of ecclesiastical authorities. In his *History of Tithes* he had brought the *jus divinum* in another of its many expressions to the test of history, and he had demonstrated its unsoundness; the same logic dictated the same conclusion when, not property, but jurisdiction was in question. In both cases, the State had fixed the limits of ecclesiastical action, and determined the practical recognition of ecclesiastical "rights." Selden speaks of Erastus with the utmost respect, and quotes the respectful language of his principal opponent, Beza, in evidence of his merits as a theologian. He protests energetically against the notion that Erastus was the originator of the views he advocated, and objects with justice to the fashion of stigmatising all who shared his opinions as to the human origin of excommunication by the scornful name Erastians, or even Colemannites, after Dr. Coleman, who represented that opinion in the Westminster Assembly; for though that was the contention of Erastus, yet it was not his invention, and had indeed been the assumption of English law from the earliest times. In truth, Selden combined in his Erastianism the knowledge of the constitutional lawyer with the anti-ecclesiastical sentiment of the scholar, and the intellectual audacity of the sceptic. His scorn of ecclesiastics in general, and of presbyterian ecclesiastics in particular, is always breaking through his arguments. "There's no such thing as spiritual jurisdiction; all is civil, the church's is the same with the lord mayor's."

"Presbyters have the greatest power of any clergy in the world, and gull the laity most." "When the queries were sent to the assembly concerning the *jus divinum* of presbytery, their asking time to consider them was a satire upon themselves. For if it were to be seen in the text, they might quickly turn to the place, and shew us it. Their delaying to answer makes us think there is no such thing there. They do just as you have seen a fellow do at a tavern reckoning, when he should come to pay his reckoning he puts his hands into his pockets, and keeps a grabbing, and a fumbling, and a shaking, at last tells you he has left his money at home; when all the company knew at first he had no money there, for every man can quickly find his own money." "Christ suffered Judas to take the communion. Those ministers that keep their parishioners from it, because they will not do as they will have them, revenge rather than reform. No man can tell whether I am fit to receive the sacrament: for though I were fit the day before, when he examined me: at least appeared so to him: yet how can he tell what sin I have committed that night, or the next morning, or what impious, atheistical thoughts I may have about me, when I am approaching to the very table?" These, and many similar utterances in the latest published and best known of Selden's works, indicate something more than the relentless lucidity of an unusually lucid understanding: they are pointed with the bitterness of intellectual resentment. The *Table Talk* is a curiously faithful summary of its author's mind,

JOHN SELDEN

as expressed in his voluminous and erudite writings. It is odd to think of Selden subscribing the covenant with the rest in S. Margaret's Church. His singularly handsome face must have worn a more than commonly sardonic expression as he affixed his name to the famous document, which might be fairly described as the formal statement of all he most disliked in politics and in religion. He certainly was an uncomfortable person in that company of divines. "The Assembly met with many difficulties," observes Fuller, "some complaining of Mr. Selden, that, advantaged by his skill in antiquity, common law, and the oriental tongues, he employed them rather to pose than profit, perplex than inform, the members thereof, in the fourteen queries he propounded : whose intent therein was to humble the *jure-divino*-ship of presbytery : which, though hinted and held forth, is not so made out in scripture, but being too scant on many occasions, it must be pieced with prudential additions. This great scholar, not over-loving of any (and least of these) clergymen, delighted himself in raising of scruples for the vexing of others: and some stick not to say, that those who will not feed on the flesh of God's word cast most bones to others, to break their teeth therewith."[1]

---

[1] *Church History*, sub anno 1644.

VII

On November 30th, 1654, Selden died, attended, if we may credit a probable story, by his friend the learned puritan, Archbishop Ussher, and declaring that "at that time he could not recollect any passage out of infinite books and manuscripts he was master of wherein he could rest his soul, save out of the holy Scriptures, wherein the most remarkable passage that lay upon his spirit was Titus ii. 11–14." It is a notable and characteristic preference of a passage which exalts the moral power and immortal hope of Christ's religion. Three years before, THOMAS HOBBES, his contemporary[1] and intimate, had published the *Leviathan*, a treatise which carried the Erastian principle to conclusions which Erastus himself would never have allowed, and which have been justly held to be inconsistent with Christianity itself. The book appeared with a frontispiece which indicated its principal contention. The State is symbolised by a giant man, whose body is made up of many small ones. The Colossus is crowned, and holds a sword in its right hand, and a crozier in its left, and it rises out of a country with a city in the foreground, which it dominates and protects.

---

[1] Selden was born in 1584; Hobbes in 1588.

Above is written the description of Leviathan in the Book of Job: "*Non est potestas super terram quae comparetur ei,*" and below the space is divided into three columns, that on the left, underneath the sword, represents the symbols of the civil power: a castle, a crown, a cannon, a sheaf of arms, and a battle; that on the left, underneath the crozier, represents the symbols of the ecclesiastical power: a church, a mitre, a thunderbolt, logic, and a court or assembly of clergy; that in the centre contains the title of the book. The suggestion is apparent and unmistakable. The State is indivisibly one, the Church is incontestably subject. Excommunication is as much Leviathan's weapon as the cannon; Leviathan smites his enemies by the decisions of his ecclesiastics as truly as by the weapons of his soldiers. There is no power but Leviathan; the powers that be are ordained of Leviathan. The picture inevitably suggests comparison with the well-known frontispiece of the Great Bible, ascribed to Holbein. Henry VIII. has the place of Leviathan, and the artist has followed a similar arrangement. The sovereigns delegate their powers to the officials of Church and State, but the whole spirit of the pictures is different. The one is personal, the other impersonal; the one is religious, the other is secular. The one indicates the apotheosis of the king, the other the rationalising of the monarchy; the one is Erastian in the sense of Cranmer, the other is Erastian in the sense of Hobbes. In the chapter, "*Of power Ecclesiastical*," Hobbes starts with the postulate that Christ bestowed on the Church no coercive power, but only a power to proclaim the gospel and to persuade men to accept it. Coercive power was by Christ's ordinance the sole attribute of the king, or other "sovereign representative of the commonwealth." Hence it follows that no part of the Christian system can be enforced except by the civil power: and, when the civil power itself became Christian, such enforcement followed as a matter of course. But the right to determine what doctrines and disciplines should be enforced was inseparable from the power to enforce them. This had been the case with the heathen; it did not cease to be the case when the heathen had become Christian. "Therefore Christian kings are still the supreme pastors of their people, and have power to ordain what pastors they please, to teach the Church, that is, to teach the people committed to their charge." In truth, all the powers inherent in the Church are vested in the Christian sovereign, for the Christian sovereign is "the Church by representation." He alone executes his office "*jure divino*," all others act "*jure civili*." "And therefore none but kings can put into their titles (a mark of their submission to God only) *Dei gratiâ Rex*, *etc*. Bishops ought to say in the beginning of their mandates, 'By the favour of the king's Majesty, bishop of such a diocese'; or as civil ministers, 'In His Majesty's Name.' For in saying, *Divinâ providentiâ*, which is the same with *Dei gratiâ*, though disguised, they deny to have received their authority from the civil state, and slyly slip off the collar of their civil subjection, contrary to the unity and defence of the commonwealth." Hobbes does not shrink from the full consequences of his theory. The Christian sovereign has authority "not only to preach (which perhaps no man will deny), but also to baptize, and to administer the sacrament, etc." He is absolute legislator over the Church, and its supreme executive officer. "In sum, he hath the supreme power in all causes, as well ecclesiastical as civil, as far as concerneth actions, and words, for those only are known, and may be accused; and of that which cannot be accused, there is no judge at all, but God, that knoweth the heart. And these rights are incident to all sovereigns, whether monarchs or assemblies: for they that are the representants of a Christian people, are representants of the Church: for a church and a commonwealth of Christian people, are the same thing."

To the obvious question, what securities his theory offers for the Christianity of the sovereign,

Hobbes makes answer in a curiously cynical discussion, "*Of what is necessary for a man's reception into the Kingdom of Heaven.*" Nothing is necessary but faith in Christ and obedience to laws. The one is internal and invisible, and under the worst circumstances Christians "have the licence that Naaman had, and need not put themselves into danger for it"; the other is summed up in obedience to the laws of God, which are only the laws of Nature, "whereof the principal is, that we should not violate our faith, that is, a commandment to obey our civil sovereigns, which we constituted over us, by mutual pact one with another." The Erastianism of Hobbes is plainly and all but confessedly non-Christian. Dr. Gardiner observes that "the historian is mainly interested in the *Leviathan* as a sign of reaction against prevailing beliefs."[1] We may add that the extravagance of those beliefs must indeed have been great which could explain so extravagant a reaction. The book raised a storm of opposition. Baxter names it among the causes which induced him to write his unfortuate *Holy Commonwealth*.[2] Bramhall wrote a series of treatises, exposing and denouncing

---

[1] *v. History of the Commonwealth and Protectorate*, vol. ii. p. 4.

[2] *v. Autobiography*, i. p. 118: "But the book which hath furnished my enemies with matter of reviling (which none must dare to answer) is my *Holy Commonwealth*. The occasion of it was this . . . Mr. Hobbs his *Leviathan* had pleased many."

his errors.[1] Thorndike was hardly less copious in the same task.[2] But the *Leviathan* was only the more read for the onslaughts made upon it. Pepys relates under the year 1668 that "Hobbs's *Leviathan*" was "now mightily called for"; and that he had to give 24*s*. for a second-hand copy originally published for 8*s*.; a new copy cost 30*s*., "it being a book the bishops will not let be printed again." It was, in truth, Hobbes who gave to Erastianism the definitely unfavourable sense which the term has ever since carried in the usage of religious men: for everywhere Hobbism was assumed to be essentially identical with Erastianism, and the Hobbesian principles, as Bramhall argued in his *Catching of Leviathan*, were "destructive to Christianity and all religion."

VIII

In truth, the Erastian controversy, so far as the original issue of excommunication was concerned, had lost practical importance and degenerated into a tiresome logomachy. For there was really no longer any question of an independent coercive power in

---

[1] These are collected in vol. iv. of Bramhall's *Works* (Library of Anglo-Catholic Theology).
[2] *v. Works* (Anglo-Catholic Library).

the Church. The rise of the dissenters, in the modern sense, went far to paralyse ecclesiastical discipline. Excommunication could never again carry its old dreadful suggestion, while the excommunicate from one Church was, by that very title, the welcome recruit of another. The machinery remained, but it was no longer effectively used, though for a few years after the Restoration the practice of excommunicating for moral offences lingered. Thus, for example, in the parish register of Barking, in Essex, there is a list of such excommunicates in the early years of Charles II., and probably in the country districts similar lists may yet be found among the parish papers of the period. Ecclesiastical discipline, obsolete everywhere else, survived in the island-diocese of Sodor and Man far into the eighteenth century, but the circumcumstances, personal and local, which made such survival possible, were not found elsewhere. As late as 1735 Bishop WILSON understood Erastianism in its true, original sense as a denial of the coercive authority of the Church. After enumerating some recent crimes in the island, he proceeds : " I cannot but ascribe this surpassing growth of wickedness . . . to the great contempt that of late has been put upon the discipline of the Church, even by some in authority, whose duty it had been to have countenanced it, as it is the law of Christians as

Christians. But Erastianism and wickedness go hand in hand and prevail."[1]

The doctrine of Erastus with respect to excommunication had always, as Selden maintained, been implied in the practice of the English State; it became again, after the Restoration, what it had been before—the avowed doctrine of the Anglican divines. JEREMY TAYLOR, for example, argues that "it is not lawful for the ecclesiastical power to excommunicate Christian princes or the supreme civil power"; and, though he concedes that a bishop "not only may, but in some cases must," refuse "to administer the holy communion to princes of a scandalous and evil life,"[2] yet he seems to admit that if the prince, thus refused, persists in desiring to communicate, "the bishop hath nothing else to do but to pray, and weep, and willingly to minister."

---

[1] *Life of Bishop Wilson*, by Keble, vol. ii. p. 773 (Library of Anglo-Catholic Theology).

[2] Jeremy Taylor's words are ambiguous, and I am not sure that I take his meaning. "For whatsoever is in the ecclesiastical hand by divine right, is as applicable to him that sits upon the throne, as to him that sits upon the dunghill. But then the refusing it must be only by admonition and caution, by fears and denunciations evangelical, by telling him his unfitness to communicate, and his danger if he do; but if, after this separation by way of sentence and proper ministry, the prince will be communicated, the bishop hath nothing else to do but to pray, and weep, and willingly to minister." This must be compared with other passages, and interpreted in the light of Anglican practice (*v. Works*, vol. xiii. p. 598 f. Heber's edition.)

Erastus would certainly have endorsed such a statement as the following : " The ecclesiastical state hath no proper coercion by divine right, but is a minister of the divine coercion, of spiritual promises and threatenings; their power is spiritual and internal, it hath its effort [? effect] upon the spirit, and not upon the outer man, and therefore is to proceed by methods fitted to the spirit, that is, by reason and argument, by the fear of God, and the terror of His threatenings, by the love of God and the invitation of His promises. But all the ministries and compulsions about the external is the gift and leave of princes. . . ."

Jeremy Taylor, in common with all the Anglican divines of his age, was preoccupied with the fear of civil sedition as commended, disguised, and advanced by religious zeal. Public reproof of kings can hardly fail to diminish their dignity in the eyes of the people, and to do this is to raise the sleeping dragon of popular disaffection. " But how and if the people be as zealous as the priest, and think it lawful to call their king by all the names of reproach, which they hear in the sermons of the ministers ? And if the bishop calls a spade a spade, it is very possible the people may do so too, for they are soon taught to despise their rulers. . . ."

This is the timidity of panic, not the reasoning of moral philosophy. Jeremy Taylor was far too genuine a Christian to be satisfied with his own conclusions, and the whole treatment of the subject has a suggestive aspect of vacillation and misgiving. The *Ductor Dubitantium*, or *Rule of Conscience*, was dedicated by its author to Charles II., and in its treatment of that worthless profligate the Anglican Church acted on the time-serving principles which inspire the passages we have quoted. A single extract from EVELYN's *Diary* will show to what lengths of degrading complacency the Church proceeded. "[1684] Easter day. The Bishop of Rochester preached before the King; after which his Majesty, accompanied with three of his natural sons, the Dukes of Northumberland, Richmond, and St. Alban's (sons of Portsmouth, Cleveland, and Nelly) went up to the altar; the three boys entering before the King within the rails, at the right hand, and three Bishops on the left: London (who officiated), Durham, and Rochester, with the Sub-Dean, Dr. Holder. The King, kneeling before the altar, making his offering, the Bishops first received, and then his Majesty: after which he retired to a canopied seat on the right hand. Note, there was perfume burnt before the office began." That service, in spite of its parade of bishops and incense, was a triumph of Erastianism; and Bishop Wilson's dictum is justified, "Erastianism and wickedness go hand in hand and prevail."

Perhaps an even more instructive example is provided by the infamous measure, which directly seized on the Holy Sacrament and bent it to the service of a political end. The Test Act of 1673 is the extremest example of Erastianism which our national record preserves. In that measure the Church tacitly, nay eagerly, yielded up to the State its spiritual heritage, to be used as a weapon against civic treason. If any proof be needed of the spiritual deadness, which is the true and unfailing consequence of Erastianism, it may be found in the amazing and disgraceful fact that the Anglican hierarchy for generations clung to the Test Act as the very palladium of Anglicanism. It will be sufficiently evident that, if this be a true account of Erastianism, the name is more often than not misapplied. The relations of Church and State in an old Christian country must necessarily take the form of working compromise in many respects, for there are facts which cannot be ignored, and ought to be fairly and frankly given their due weight when the administration of the Church is in question. The citizens are in many cases also Christians; the laws are the depositaries, expositions, and instruments of Christian principles; the system of the Church is, in a hundred ways, incorporated into the system of the State; interests, not distinctively spiritual and not formally or specifically ecclesiastical, enter the sanctuary when a Christian Church has once taken possession of a national life. From all these conditions of existence there is no escape; in them there is no necessary Erastianism. There would be nothing inherently Erastian in a parliamentary revision of the Prayer-book, though it might be unconstitutional, and would almost certainly be unsatisfactory. A church which admits notoriously immoral persons to Holy Communion is properly and apparently Erastian. There is no validity in the common claim of the clergy to monopolise the name and attributes of the Church. No official class can really absorb into itself the powers of the society, from which it draws its being; and if that society be,—as is the case of the Christian Church,—divinely originated, that circumstance implies no exception to the general rule. The original elements of historic Christianity are few, and they are as much beyond the manipulation of the "Church" as of the "State." Convocation may be as Erastian as Parliament, and has a far inferior record of religious legislation.

To sum up. Erastianism, as the protest against attaching civil penalties to spiritual censures, has rooted itself among us as an axiom of ecclesiastical politics. Erastianism, as a denial of the obligation resting on the Church of Christ to assert the moral conditions of Christian membership, has revealed in experience its inherent infidelity to fundamental Christian principle, and is repudiated by all to whom the religion of Christ is something more than an earth-born tradition, or a serviceable factor in secular politics.

Casuistry

Richard Hooker	. .	1554–1600
William Perkins	. .	1558–1602
Joseph Hall .	. .	1574–1656
William Ames .	. .	1576–1633
Robert Sanderson	. .	1587–1663
Thomas Barlow	. .	1607–1691
Jeremy Taylor .	. .	1613–1667
Richard Baxter .	. .	1615–1691
Thomas Ken .	. .	1637–1711
Gilbert Burnet .	. .	1643–1715

I

THE Reformation was an indiscriminating process for the most part; it swept away much that, when the first ardours of zeal had subsided, men found cause to regret. Thus in respect of the ancient and complicated system of moral discipline, the most abused, perhaps, and the least defensible of all the characteristic features of the medieval Church, there was a sudden, violent, and complete transition effected by the Reformers. They moved almost at a stride from the control of the confessional to that absolute independence of external moral discipline which has become the distinguishing mark of Protestant society. This transition, apparent at once in the region of practice, was but slowly and reluctantly admitted in that of ecclesiastical theory. All the Protestant Churches provided some machinery to take the place of the medieval penitential system. A voluntary and consultative confessional was set up, and Christians were urged to make use of it ; more or less vague assurances as to the value of ministerial absolution were offered to penitents, and no doubt there were many to whom they brought spiritual comfort ; but, for the mass of men, the definite repudiation of the sacerdotal character of the ministry, and the explicit assertion of the right of private judgment, implied the disappearance of external moral discipline, apart, of course, from the restraints of public law. The effect on morality was not good. Abrupt abolitions of disciplinary systems are always very precarious and perilous experiments, and in this case the character of the system—detailed, compulsory, universal—enhanced the risks of abolition. Private virtue had from time immemorial been subjected to vigilant and continuous official oversight ; and, as an inevitable consequence, it had become, for the multitude of men, a strangely dependent thing ; the cessation of official oversight drew with it, in countless cases, the failure of personal morality. Moreover, the confessional of the medieval Church had reposed on an implicit faith in certain dogmas, sacerdotal and sacramental, which, so far as the mass of Christians was concerned, were so firmly rooted that almost incredible practical abuses and the grotesquest theoretical paradoxes were powerless to affect them. These dogmas perished wherever the Reformation prevailed, and, in place of the old, unquestioned, and coherent system of belief, men found themselves committed to a distracting series of speculations and disputations, theological, moral, political, which seemed to bring the very existence of religious truth into question and to destroy all firm foundation for conduct. There was much failure of faith, much disorder of life, much distress of mind. Under these circumstances it is not surprising to find that serious Christians, in all sections of the Protestant Church, turned their thoughts towards discovering some remedy for these mischiefs. In point of fact, we find a twofold movement in progress. On the one hand, there was the sustained attempt to formulate and practically enforce a new conception of the Christian Church as a society exercising moral discipline over its members; on the other hand, there was the effort to discover in Scripture and reason a new casuistry for the guidance of Christians, which should take the place of the canon law and the confessor's direction.

This twofold movement proceeded throughout reformed Europe, but in England, as might have been expected, it took a form and course of its own. It is to be observed that there was in progress at the same time, and connected with the same causes, that great reform and redirection of the confessional at the hands of the Jesuits, which was the prevailing instrument of the counter-Reformation, and has transformed the aspect and spirit of the Roman Church. At every point the Protestant casuists are found to be taking account of their Jesuit contemporaries, and the whole disciplinary movement, Roman and Reformed, must take its place in a philosophic view of the seventeenth century as a single phenomenon. But though the phenomenon was one and the same, being, in truth, the attempt to bring again under the control of the moral law the populations of Christendom, which, under the revolutionary conditions of the time, had in many directions broken away from all moral restraints, yet it proceeded on very different principles in the Roman and in the Protestant spheres, and commonly took the aspect of avowed contradiction. Casuistry in the mouth of a Protestant does not mean the same thing as in that of a Roman Catholic. Protestant casuistry is primarily intended for the use of perplexed persons, and serves more or less sufficiently the purpose of a living guide: it therefore discusses principles, and indicates the general line of their practical application; but abstains from elaborate discussions, avoids unlikely cases, and everywhere makes appeal to the conscience and reason of the perplexed, as properly responsible in the sequel for whatever decision is taken. It exhibits the reticence, reasonableness, and responsibility of public teaching. The writings of the English casuists are in no need of the apologies for inevitable indecency and ethical paradox which are advanced in defence of the casuistry of the Jesuits: they might be read from the pulpit, or to a family circle. It is hardly an exaggeration to say that they were meant to be so read. The practice of private confession may or may not be recommended by the casuist: it certainly has no necessary connection with his casuistry. The Roman Catholic casuistry, on the contrary, is inseparable from the confessional: it is the private manual of the priest, designed to equip him for his work in hearing confessions. Not the morally perplexed are his concern so much as the morally polluted. Perplexity may be limited to a single point, but pollution has endless ramifications, and in determining its extent and gravity, the doctor of the soul can recognise no limits to the information he may require. The Protestant casuistry recognises the normal and ultimate judge of conduct to be the individual Christian conscience, illumined by the Holy Spirit and informed by the gospel, and proposes the help of the Christian ministry as one of the means by which the conscience may be strengthened for its own incommunicable task. The Roman Catholic casuistry assumes that "in the confessional the priest holds the place of God, and is obliged to utter a decision on all matters submitted to him: his jurisdiction extends over every act of life, and decides not only the destiny of the soul, but the legality of whatever the penitent may do or leave undone; no transaction is too complex, no social relation too delicate, to be withdrawn from his judgment; and on it may depend the future of the faithful both in this world and the next, for the Church assumes the direction of the lives as well as of the souls of its subjects."[1]

From the necessities of so immense a task, casuistry of the elaborated and unblushing type which Blaise Pascal exposed to perpetual contempt took its origin. "Papal and conciliar decrees cover but a fraction of the cases on which the confessor must act, and even in these the application of general rules to special cases is mostly a task of

---

[1] *v. Auricular Confession and Indulgences*, Henry Charles Lea, LL.D., vol. ii. p. 285. [London, 1896.]

extreme nicety, so that for the most part he must trust to the opinions of the experts who have exhaustively investigated law and morals, and endeavoured to reason out every possible contingency in the boundless intricacy of human thoughts and passions and actions."[1] But when once free play is permitted to the human mind, a conflict of opinions is certain to arise. This was notoriously the case within the casuistic sphere. The masters of moral science were not agreed, and the confessor, depending on their guidance, was in worse case than ever. A way out of the ecclesiastical *impasse* was found by the famous theory of probabilism, which took its origin in the sixteenth century, and in the hands of the Jesuits pushed its way to general acceptance in spite of the most vehement opposition, and of scandals persistent and amazing. JEREMY TAYLOR, in the preface to his famous casuistic treatise, *Ductor Dubitantium, or the Rule of Conscience*," published at the Restoration with a dedication to Charles II., dwells on the false method of the Roman casuists, and the unfortunate moral consequences to which it led. After denouncing the " heaps of prodigious propositions and rules of conscience their doctors have given us," and alluding to that pervading and persistent indecency

---

[1] *Ibid.*

which is the worst feature of Roman casuistry, he proceeds to challenge "the strange manner of their answerings." "That which I suppose to be of greatest consideration is, that the casuists of the Roman Church take these things for resolution and answer to questions of conscience, which are spoken by an authority that is not sufficient . . . . And the mischief of this is further yet discernible, if we consider that they determine their greatest and most mysterious cases oftentimes by no other argument but the saying of some few of their writers . . . The effect of these uncertain principles and unsteady conduct of questions is this; that though by violence and force they have constrained and thrust their churches into a union of faith, like beasts into a pound, yet they have made their cases of conscience and the actions of their lives unstable as the face of the waters, and immeasurable as the dimensions of the moon: by which means their confessors shall be enabled to answer according to every man's humour, and no man shall depart sad from their penitential chairs, and themselves shall take or give leave to any thing; concerning which I refer the reader to the books and letters written by their parties of Port-Royal, and to their own weak answers and vindications." Jeremy Taylor, therefore, finding the Roman casuistry unsuitable for English use, thinks it "necessary that cases of conscience should be written over anew, and established upon better principles, and proceed in more sober and satisfying methods," and sets himself to do this in his treatise. He intends his book to be in the hands of laymen, but does not suppose that it will provide them with an adequate substitute for the guidance of the clergy. "For I intend here to offer to the world a general instrument of moral theology, by the rules and measures of which, the guides of souls may determine the particulars that shall be brought before them: and those who love to inquire, may also find their duty so described, that unless their duties be complicated with laws, and civil customs and secular interests, men that are wise may guide themselves in all their proportions of conscience: but if their case be indeed involved, they need the conduct of a spiritual guide, to untie the intrigue, and state the question, and apply the respective rules to the several parts of it: for though I have set them down all in their proper places relating to their several matters, yet when a question requires the reason of many rules, it is not every hand that can apply them: men will for ever need a living guide; and a wise guide of souls will, by some of these rules, be enabled to answer most cases that shall occur." There was an ascetic strain in Jeremy Taylor which gives a distinctive tone to his writings, and a strong professional sense, which makes him always set the position of the clergy high, but the important thing to notice is the decisive repudiation of Roman principles and methods with which he prefaces his great casuistic treatise. Anglican casuistry may be good, or bad: one thing is certain, it is a home-grown thing, and has little in common with the casuistry of the Church of Rome.

II

In the præ-Laudian Church, especially among the Puritans, no casuist was more highly regarded than "that famous and worthy minister of Christ in the University of Cambridge, MR. WILLIAM PERKINS," whose life was almost exactly conterminous with the reign of Elizabeth. In his quaintly fascinating treatise, *The Holy and Profane State*, Fuller chooses Perkins as the type of "the faithful minister," and describes him with evident admiration. In his youth he had been addicted to drunkenness, but, being converted, he became a rigid Calvinist. His work as a preacher began among the prisoners in the Castle of Cambridge, and was speedily extended to others until it exercised a distinct and powerful influence on the general life of the University. Perkins, in fact, was a sixteenth-century Charles Simeon. It is evident that he was a notable and winning person. "Of a ruddy complexion, very fat and corpulent, lame of his right hand," he arrested the gaze of the undergraduates, who found him, after the first stiffness had worn away, "of a cheerful nature and pleasant disposition," "merry and very familiar." And yet he must have been severe enough in the pulpit. "He would pronounce the word *damn* with such an emphasis as left a doleful echo in his auditors' ears a good while after; and when Catechist of Christ College, in expounding the Commandments, applied them so home, able almost to make his hearers' hearts fall down and hairs to stand upright. But in his older age he altered his voice, and remitted much of his former rigidness; often professing that to preach mercy was that proper office of the ministers of the Gospel." He was gifted with the power of easy and lucid utterance, and he facilitated attention by a simple but logical arrangement of his materials. "An excellent surgeon he was at jointing a broken soul, and at stating of a doubtful conscience." "Perkins's reputation as a teacher during the closing years of his life was unrivalled in the University, and few students of theology quitted Cambridge without having sought to profit in some measure by his instruction; while as a writer he continued to be studied throughout the seventeenth century as an authority but little inferior to Hooker and Calvin."[1]

An excellent example of Perkins's casuistic method is *The Whole Treatise of the Cases of Conscience, distinguished into 3 books*. It is on many counts interesting that he, like Jeremy Taylor, distinctly advises the practice of private confession, though under conditions far enough removed from those which obtain in the Roman Church.

"In the troubles of the conscience," he says, "it is meet and convenient that there should always be used a private confession. For James saith, 'Confess your sins one to another, and pray for one another,' thereby signifying that confession in this case is to be used as a thing most requisite. For in all reason the physician must know the disease before he can apply the remedy: and the grief of the heart will not be discerned unless it be manifested by the confession of the party diseased; and for this cause also in the grief of conscience, the *scruple*, that is, the thing that troubleth the conscience, must be known. Nevertheless, in private confession, these caveats must be observed. First, it must not be urged as a thing simply or absolutely necessary, without which there can be no salvation.

---

[1] *Dictionary of National Biography*, vol. xlv. p. 7.

Again, it is not fit that confession should be of all sins, but only of the scruple itself, that is, of that or those sins alone which do trouble and molest the conscience. Thirdly, though confession may be made to any man ('Confess one to another,' saith James), yet is it especially to be made to the prophets and ministers of the Gospel. For they, in likelihood of all other men, in respect of their places and gifts, are the fittest and best able to instruct, correct, comfort, and inform the weak and wounded conscience. Lastly, the person to whom it is made must be a man of trust and fidelity, able and willing to keep secret things that are revealed, yea, to bury them, as it were, in the grave of oblivion, for 'love covereth a multitude of sins.'"[1]

In his treatise, *Of the Nature and Practise of Repentance*, Perkins speaks even more decisively: "As for confession of sins to men," he says, "it is not to be used but in two cases. First, when some offence is done to our neighbour: secondly, when ease and comfort is sought for trouble of conscience."[2] In another treatise, *A Salve for a Sick Man, or A Treatise containing the nature, differences, and kinds of death, as also the right manner of dying well*, he states and repudiates the Roman

---

[1] *v. Works*, vol. ii. p. 2. 1609.
[2] *Ibid.*, vol. i. p. 461.

doctrine of "Sacramental Confession." "Confession of our sins, and that unto men, was never denied of any; the question only is of the manner and order of making confession. And for this cause we must put a great difference between Popish shrift and the confession of which St. James speaketh. For he requires only a confession of that or those sins which lie upon a man's conscience when he is sick; but the Popish doctrine requireth a particular enumeration of all a man's sins."[1] It is sufficiently evident that Perkins had little sympathy with the confessional in the Roman sense. His lofty doctrine as to the conscience could not be reconciled to an institution which inevitably lowered the prestige and limited the authority of the individual conscience. "Inferior authority," he says in his *Treatise of Conscience*, "cannot bind the superior; now the courts of men and their authority are under conscience. For God in the heart of every man hath erected a tribunal seat, and in his stead he hath placed neither saint nor angel, nor any other creature whatsoever, but conscience itself, who therefore is the highest judge that is, or can be, under God; by whose directions also courts are kept and laws are made." "If a man being to make an unknown journey should find one that would go with him, and show him

---

[1] *Ibid.*, vol. i. pp. 496–8.

the way, and all the turnings thereof, he could not but take it for a point of courtesy. Well, we are pilgrims in this world, our life is our journey. God also hath appointed our conscience to be our companion and guide, to show us what course we may take and what we may not."[1]

This note of the supremacy of conscience is sustained throughout the discussions of specific "cases," and constitutes them, what indeed casuistic writing rarely is found to be, really invigorating to the moral character of the student. Perkins transmitted to his disciples this tradition of case-morality, and it is the honourable distinction of his school that, in the main, it continued loyal to his teaching. Perhaps the most widely influential of the Puritan casuists who owed their training to Perkins was WILLIAM AMES (1576-1633), long known in casuistic discussions as Amesius. His stiff Puritanism and plain speech destroyed a promising academic career, and brought him into collision with the ecclesiastical authorities. Even the Calvinistic Archbishop Abbot described him as no obedient son of the Church, being a rebel against her authority. For ten years he held the professorship of theology at Franeker with great distinction, "his reputation as a theologian and his ability as a teacher attracting students not only

---
[1] *Ibid.*, vol. i. pp. 523, 530.

from all parts of the United Provinces, but also from Hungary, Poland, and Russia." In the year before his death, *i.e.* in 1632, Ames published the work which has made his reputation with posterity, *De Conscientia, ejus Jure et Casibus*. "It was an elaborate attempt to make the application of the general principles of Christian morality more certain and clear in relation to particular cases, and served to make the name of 'AMESIUS' classical in the schools of moral philosophy. His biographer speaks of it as removing a reproach from the learning of Protestantism, and relieving its teachers from the necessity of resorting to 'the Philistines' for assistance in the determination of nice points in cases of conscience."[1] "Within the compass of a small 12mo volume," writes Orme of this book, "is comprised a larger portion of practical and scriptural instruction than in almost any book that I know. He is remarkably accurate in his definitions, and had a power of compression utterly unknown to Baxter."[2] In his interesting and characteristic "Advertisement" to his lengthy treatise, *A Christian Directory, or a sum of Practical Theology and Cases of Conscience*, Baxter pays homage to the casuistic labours of Amesius. The bulk of this treatise was, he says, written

---

[1] *Dict. of Nat. Biog.*, vol. i. p. 357.
[2] *v. Life of Baxter*, p. 544, note.

in 1664 and 1665, when he "was forbidden by the law to preach, and when he had been long separated far from his library and from all books, saving an inconsiderable parcel which wandered with him where he went." At that time his only casuist was Amesius. Baxter thinks that the absence of books may not be wholly disadvantageous. "It may be some little advantage to [the reader] that he hath no transcript of any man's books, which he had before; but the product of some experience, with a naked, unbiassed perception of the matter or things themselves." He sums up the situation with respect to English casuistry in the paragraph in which he states the objects with which he himself put his hand to the task. He wrote "that the younger and more unfurnished and unexperienced sort of ministers might have a promptuary at hand for practical resolutions and directions on the subjects that they have need to deal in. And though Sayrus and Fragoso have done well, I would not have us under a necessity of going to the Romanists for our ordinary supplies. Long have our divines been wishing for some fuller casuistical tractate: Perkins began well: Bishop Sanderson hath done excellently 'de juramento'; Amesius hath exceeded all, though briefly. Mr. David Dickson hath put more of our English cases about the state of sanctification into Latin than ever was done before him. Bishop Jeremy Taylor hath in two folios but begun the copious performance of the work. And still men are calling for more, which I have attempted, hoping that others will come after and do better than we all." But Baxter did not write only for the clergy, he designed his "Directory" for "the more judicious masters of families, who may choose and read such parcels to their families as at any time the case requireth."[1] The work itself is marked by the great merits, and also by the well-known faults, of its author. Perhaps, considered as a practical guide to conduct, it is the most serviceable book in the language. In spite of its diffuseness, and tendency to excessive subdivision, it is always shrewd, reasonable, and high-minded; besides being, what casuistic treatises very frequently are not, eminently readable.

PERKINS, AMES, and BAXTER form the trinity of Puritan casuists, who are matched by the three casuistic bishops, HALL, SANDERSON, and TAYLOR. It is very noteworthy that there is no essential divergence either of principle or of method between Puritans and Anglicans on the subject of moral theology. The practice of confession probably connected itself in the Anglican mind with a theory of the ministry, which the Puritans did not allow; but

---

[1] *v. Works*, ed. Orme, vol. ii.

this connection was for the most part unexpressed, and as to the practical wisdom of consulting a spiritual guide, the Puritan, who regarded the ordained minister as the Christian prophet, came not a whit behind the Anglican, who regarded him as a Christian priest. Both repudiated the Roman confessional with equal decision.

III

BISHOP HALL (1574–1656) enjoyed among his contemporaries a reputation as a preacher, divine, and devotional writer which has thrown into obscurity his character as a casuist, but that he was no mean proficient in this respect also will be at once apparent to the student of his *Resolutions and decisions of divers practical cases of conscience in continual use among men*,[1] published in 1648, with the official licence of John Downham, expressed in highly laudatory terms. The author in a brief preface justifies his method. He has limited himself to those practical cases which are of most common use, because error in respect of them is most widely mischievous. "These I have selected out of many, and having turned over divers casuists have pitched

---

[1] This treatise is printed in vol. vii. of Hall's works, edited by Wynter. [Oxford, 1863.]

upon these decisions, which I hold most conformable to enlightened reason and religion. Sometimes I follow them, and sometimes I leave them for a better guide." The treatise is divided into four decades of cases. (1) Cases of Profit and Traffick. (2) Cases of Life and Liberty. (3) Cases of Piety and Religion. (4) Cases Matrimonial. To the last four additional cases are appended. At the end is *An Advertisement to the Reader*, which is not without interest. "I have been earnestly moved by some judicious friends to go on with this subject, and to make up a complete body of case-divinity, both practical, speculative and mixed; whereof, I confess, there is great defect in our language." This task he declines on the ground of his advanced age (he was then in his seventy-fifth year), but pledges himself to deal with such scruples as he shall meet with in his way, and to "leave the answers upon the file." The distinctive character and special excellence of English casuistry are indicated in these words. It has its origin in practical necessities, and is determined in method and limited in range by actual conditions of life. Its authors are men of affairs, heads of households, in close, habitual contact with the ordinary course of human action. It is not unworthy of notice that all the principal English casuists of the seventeenth century were married men. Hooker, Perkins, Ames,

Hall, Sanderson, Baxter, Jeremy Taylor all formed and wrote their casuistic opinions in the atmosphere of their own homes. And this circumstance goes far to explain the sanity and clean-mindedness of their discussions. The Roman casuists were always celibates, and commonly worked in the cloister. Their facts were collected, not in the healthy intercourse of ordinary society, but in the confessional. And the atmosphere of the confessional must be unhealthy and unfavourable to just views, for human nature, as exhibited in the self-revelations of remorse and the self-accusations of penitence, is necessarily abnormally bad, and the moral philosopher who accepts that version of human nature as the basis of his work will inevitably assume the worst of human action, and credit to ordinary, healthy-minded individuals something of the morbid viciousness which has given to the confessional its lurid interest. Moreover, the atmosphere affects the moral philosopher himself. A powerful and well-trained mind, continually engaged in the consideration of unwholesome aspects of human nature, deliberately committed to the logical treatment of intrinsically demoralising phenomena, must itself be injuriously affected. Even moral philosophers are also men, and cloister walls cannot shut out the incorrigible weakness of humanity. In effect, the actual character of Roman casuistry exhibits precisely the qualities which a review of the conditions under which it originates would suggest—thoroughness, extraordinary detail, rigorous logic as to arrangement, an underlying assumption everywhere sustained that men are probably more debased than they know, and (to speak the whole truth) a certain fondness for handling unclean subjects, which makes that literature the most subtly demoralising in the world.

It may be serviceable to quote the description of the Roman practice and its effect, which one who had experienced both in the double capacity of priest and penitent has left on record. Blanco White no doubt viewed the Roman system with insurmountable resentment, and the reader of the "narrative of his life" will remember the fact, but he was a singularly honest man, and there can be no doubt whatever as to the substantial truth of his statements. Speaking of Loyola's spiritual exercises, he says:—

"This was the appointed time to begin the *General Confessions*. That name is likely to lead Protestants into a mistake; for it means, not a general acknowledgment of sinfulness, but a detailed account of the previous life of the person who is to make the *general* confession. Every thought, word, and deed, nay, every doubt, every uncertainty of conscience that can be called to remembrance, must be stated to the Priest, at whose feet the self-accuser kneels during the *long* narrative. I say *long*, because the result of such a process of examination, as is carried on for four or five days, by the penitent himself, under the impression that any negligence on his part must involve him in guilt far exceeding that of all his former misdeeds, produces (in the sincere and sensitive) a morbid anxiety of which none but those who have experienced it can form an adequate notion. I will not stop to urge the grounds of a conviction, on which I have enlarged elsewhere —that auricular confession is one of the most mischievous practices of the Romanist Church. To those who are not totally ignorant of the philosophy of morals, it must be clear that such minute attention to individual faults—not to trace them to their source in the heart, but in order to ascertain whether they are *venial* or *morta* sins, according to the judgment of another man—must, in an infinite number of cases, check the development of conscience, and may totally destroy it in many. As far as my experience extends (and I have had fair opportunities of observing the effects of Romanism in myself and in many others), the evils of auricular confession increase in proportion to the sincerity with which it is practised. I know that what I am going to say will sound extremely harsh and startling to many. But I will not conceal or disguise the truth. Many, indeed, were the evils of which my subsequent period of disbelief in Christianity (a disbelief full of spite for the evils inflicted upon me in its name) was the occasion; yet I firmly believe that, but for the buffetings of that perilous storm, scarcely a remnant of the quick moral perception which God had naturally given to my mind would have escaped destruction by the emaciating poison of confession. I judge from the certain knowledge of the secret conduct of many members of the clergy, who were deemed patterns of devotion. Like those wretched slaves, I should have been permanently the worse for the custom of sinning and washing the sin away by confession. Free, however, from that debasing practice, my conscience assumed the rule, and, independently of hopes and fears, it clearly blamed what was clearly wrong, and, as it were, learned to act by virtue of its natural supremacy."[1] I think it may be said with confidence that such "general confession" as is here described receives no countenance from the Anglican casuists. It is, indeed, an interesting question how far their authority can fairly be

---

[1] *v. Life of the Rev. Joseph Blanco White.* Written by himself; edited by John William Thom, vol. i. pp. 42-4. [London, 1845.]

pleaded by the advocates of private or auricular confession. That a practice of private confession is recognised in the Prayer Book is, of course, apparent, and not seriously disputed in any quarter. But what was that practice? How far can it be urged to justify the restoration within the Anglican Church of what is to all intents and purposes the Roman institution, in its later Jesuitised form, of the confessional? The 113th Canon of 1603 prohibits the minister "under pain of irregularity" from revealing offences made known to him in confession, unless "they be such crimes as by the laws of this realm" the minister's own life might be endangered for concealing them.

Dr. Pusey in an elaborate introduction to his translation of the Abbé Gaume's *Manual for Confessors*, designed for the use of the English clergy, collected an imposing array of Anglican testimonies to the theory and practice of confession; but those testimonies, in order to be justly appraised, ought to be in every case considered in connection with the immediate purpose of the writer, and, in most cases, conditioned by his general attitude of hostility to the Roman confessional. There is, on the face of it, something oddly incongruous in making the Anglican casuists recommend a Roman Manual, for, speaking broadly, it was an agreed point among them that the Roman casuistry was unsound and demoralising. To give but a single example. Dr. Pusey gives an extract from the famous poet-preacher DONNE, who at the end of a sermon preached to the Royal Household at Whitehall in 1626 makes some reference to confession. The actual quotation as it stands in Dr. Pusey's Catena is as follows:—

"For confession, we require public confession in the congregation; and in time of sickness, upon the death-bed, we enjoin private and particular confession, if the conscience be oppressed; and if any man do think that that which is necessary for him, upon his death-bed, is necessary every time he comes to the communion, and so come to such a confession, if anything lie upon him, as often as he comes to the communion, we blame not, we dissuade not, we discounsel not, that tenderness of conscience, and that safe proceeding in that good soul." Now this passage is taken out of a polemical context. Donne is defending the Anglican system against "the Pharisees, our adversaries," *i.e.* the Roman Catholics, who "say we admit men too easily to the sacrament; without confession, without contrition, without satisfaction." Then follows the passage quoted, after which Donne goes on to gird at his adversaries again. Dr. Pusey observes that Donne "praises the tenderness of conscience which would make confession before every communion," whereas the real drift of the whole passage is not hortatory, but apologetic.[1] The controversy with Rome did undoubtedly induce in Anglicans an emphasising of such elements in the English Church as were denied to exist by the Roman enemy. For polemical purposes it was important to show that there was no part of the traditional Catholic system which the reformed Church of England did not possess, but it would be precarious to build too much on these polemical assertions. An immense amount of formal theorising and conventional exhortation go to an astonishingly small amount of appropriate practice. Private confession was practised by the Laudian clergy and by a certain number of devout lay-folk, like EVELYN,[2] who had adopted Laudian principles; but the mass of Anglicans, both clergy and laity, then, as now, did not go to confession themselves, and thought it rather an unwholesome sign in other people if they did. No doubt the theory of the confessional made way in the Church under the twofold pressure of Puritanism and Popery. Bishop Hall is appreciably more sacerdotal than Perkins, and Jeremy Taylor than Bishop Hall. The excellent KEN, in his *Manual of Prayers*

---

[1] *v.* Donne's *Works*, vol. v. p. 482–506. [London, 1839.]

[2] *v. Diary*, March 18th, 1655: "I made a visit to Dr. Jeremy Taylor, to confer with him about some spiritual matters, using him thenceforward as my ghostly father."

for the use of the Scholars of Winchester, tells his young Philotheus, quite in the style of a modern Ritualist, to go to confession to a Spiritual Guide; but we may be fairly confident that the public school-boy of the seventeenth century was no more responsive to such treatment than his compeer of our own time. Individuals here and there went to confession as they do now, and it was urged as a Christian duty by many of the clergy then as now, though far more moderately, but so far as the general practice of English churchmen went, the practice of private confession had ceased to exist. Casuistry, then, in England was developed apart from that institution and that religious habit, which on the Continent exercised a dominating influence. "*Scruples*" were the main concern of the insular divines, and these were often rather theological and ecclesiastical than, in the true sense, moral. One class of questions which has an important place in the casuistic discussions of the age was directly connected with the religious controversies which then raged with almost incredible fury.

"I was troubled this year," writes Baxter under the date 1671, "with multitudes of melancholy persons from several parts of the land, some of high quality, some of low, some very exquisitely learned, some unlearned (as I had in a great measure been above twenty years before). I know not how it came to pass, but if men fell melancholy, I must hear from them or see them (more than any physician that I know). Which I mention only for these three uses to the reader, that out of all their cases I have gathered, (1) That we must very much take heed lest we ascribe melancholy phantasms and passions to God's Spirit: for they are strange apprehensions that melancholy can cause. . . . (2) I would warn all young persons to live modestly, and keep at a sufficient distance from objects that tempt them to carnal lust, and to take heed of wanton dalliance, and the beginnings or approaches of this sin, and that they govern their thoughts and senses carefully. For I can tell them by the sad experience of many that venerous crimes leave deep wounds in the conscience. . . . (3) I advise all men to take heed of placing religion too much in fears, and tears, and scruples; or in any other kind of sorrow, but such as tendeth to raise us to a high estimation of Christ, and to the magnifying of grace, and a sweeter taste of the love of God, and to the firmer resolution against sin. . . . Reader," he adds, "I do but transcribe these three counsels for thee, from a multitude of melancholy persons' sad experiences."[1] BISHOP BURNET, with characteristic good sense, declared that these cases of melancholy were often more physical than religious.

---

[1] *Autobiography*, part iii., pp. 85–6.

"Alas! the greater part of those that think they are troubled in mind are melancholy, hypochondriacal people, who, what through some false opinions in religion, what through a foulness of the blood, occasioned by their unactive course of life, in which their minds work too much, because their bodies are too little employed, fall under dark and cloudy apprehensions—of which they can give no clear nor good account. This, in the greatest part, is to be removed by strong and chalybeate medicines: yet such persons are to be much pitied, and a little humoured in their distemper. They must be diverted from thinking too much, being too much alone, or dwelling too long on thoughts that are too hard for them to master." He directly ascribes such cases of melancholy to the fanatical religious movements of the time. "The opinion that has had the chief influence in raising these distempers has been that of praying by the Spirit—when a flame of thought, a melting in the brain, and the abounding in tender expressions, have been thought the effects of the Spirit, moving all those symptoms of warm temper. . . . If then a minister has occasion to treat any in this condition, he must make them apprehend that the heat or coldness of their brain is the effect of temper, and flows from the different state of the animal spirits, which have their diseases, their hot and their cold fits, as well as the blood has: and therefore no measure can be taken from these either to judge for or against themselves. They are to consider what are their principles and resolutions, and what is the settled course of their life: upon these they are to form sure judgments, and not upon anything that is so fluctuating and inconsistent as fits and humours."[1] Whether Burnet's diagnosis of melancholy would pass the College of Physicians I cannot say, but I am sure he was right in regarding this unhappy state as more properly related to the physical than to the spiritual condition of the sufferer.

Religious melancholy, stimulated by the fanaticism and superstition of the time, led to many tragedies of suicide: and, in this connection, we must mention the terror of Satanic action, expressed by the numerous judicial executions of witches,[2] and a revived interest in astrology, necromancy, and many similar forms of superstition. These darker aspects of that age, which constitute it perhaps the most bigotry-ridden epoch of modern history, were necessarily reflected in the "scruples," which casuistic divines were called upon to consider and determine.

---

[1] *v.* "Of the Pastoral Instructor," printed in *The Clergyman's Instructor*, pp. 175-6. [Oxford, 1855.]

[2] It is said that no less than 5,000 persons suspected of dealings with the Evil One perished in the kingdom during the Commonwealth.

ROBERT SANDERSON (1587–1663), who held the See of Lincoln for three years after the Restoration, was, perhaps, the most highly regarded of all the Laudian casuists. Laud is said to have recommended him to Charles I. specially on the ground of his excellence in all "casuistical learning," and once known to the king, he rapidly acquired great influence with him. Charles "put many cases of conscience to him," and "received such deliberate, safe, and clear solutions as gave him great content." During Sanderson's month of attendance as chaplain the good king was never absent from his sermons, and would usually say, "I carry my ears to hear other preachers, but I carry my conscience to hear Mr. Sanderson, and to act accordingly." "And this ought not to be concealed from posterity," adds Walton, "that the king thought what he spake, for he took him to be his adviser in that quiet part of his life, and he proved to be his comforter in those days of his affliction when he was under such a restraint as he apprehended himself to be in danger of death or deposing."

In 1642 Charles appointed him Regius Professor of Divinity at Oxford, where, however, he performed none of the duties of his professorship until 1646, when he delivered a course of casuistic lectures, which became famous. He began with a subject *De Juramento*, which was, in that age of political and religious unrest, a fruitful cause of perplexity. "But this learned man," writes his admiring biographer, "as he was eminently furnished with abilities to satisfy the consciences of men upon that important subject: so he wanted not courage to assert the true obligation of it, and of oaths, in a degenerate age, when men had made perjury a main part of, or at least very useful to, their religion." When the king fell into the hands of the Independents, and was permitted to have chaplains of his own choice, he sent for Sanderson, among others, and consulted him as to the parliamentary demands. "And at Dr. Sanderson's then taking his leave of His Majesty in this his last attendance on him, the king requested him to betake himself to the writing cases of conscience for the good of posterity. To which his answer was, "That he was now grown old, and unfit to write cases of conscience." But the king was so bold with him as to say, "It was the simplest answer he ever heard from Dr. Sanderson; for no young man was fit to make a judge or write cases of conscience." It was to Sanderson, together with Morley, that Charles entrusted his secret purpose "that if God ever restored him to be in a peaceable possession of his crown, he would demonstrate his repentance" for assenting to Strafford's death and to the abolition of episcopacy in Scotland "by a public confession and voluntary penance from the Tower of London, or Whitehall, to St. Paul's Church, and desire the people to intercede with God for his pardon," and Charles is said to have spent his solitude in the Isle of Wight, before the final disaster came to him, in translating Sanderson's lectures *De Juramento* into exact English. Charles I., with no other consciousness of political fault than this, and no other purpose of showing his repentance than a procession barefoot through the streets of London begging his people's prayers that he might be forgiven the two acts which they almost all would certainly hold to be the wisest he ever performed, is an interesting but hardly an edifying spectacle. Casuistic guidance does not appear to have done much to clear and strengthen his naturally crooked intelligence or to awaken and direct his curiously obtuse conscience, obtuse, and yet as curiously sensitive, the conscience in fact of a narrow-natured man in a great and difficult position confused by the twin errors of absolutism and superstition. Sanderson's close intimacy with the Royal Martyr marked him out as a spiritual guide for all who revered the Royal Martyr's memory, and found themselves, in consequence, strangely perplexed by the revolution in which the king had perished. And his situation as one of the few leading royalist ecclesiastics who remained in the country made recourse to him for spiritual counsel comparatively easy. "In this time of his poor but contented privacy of life, his casuistical learning, peaceful moderation and sincerity, became so remarkable that there were many that applied themselves to him for resolution in perplexed cases of conscience, some known to him and many not, some requiring satisfaction by conference, others by letters; so many, that his life became almost as restless as their minds." Some of these cases of conscience were collected and published. Walton enumerates eight which may be quoted as showing the nature of the questions which exercised men's minds at that time. They are the following:—

(1) Of the sabbath.
(2) Marrying with a recusant.
(3) Of unlawful love.
(4) Of a military life.
(5) Of scandal.
(6) Of a bond taken in the king's name.
(7) Of the engagement.
(8) Of a rash vow.

About the year 1655 Walton relates that he fell in with Sanderson "accidentally in London in sad-coloured clothes, and, God knows, far from being costly," that as it came on to rain they took shelter together, and, the rain increasing, were finally forced "into a cleanly house, where they had bread, cheese, ale, and a fire for their ready money." Walton seized the opportunity for learning the famous doctor's opinions as to the existing religious confusion; nor was Sanderson averse to speaking freely to one who was so well known as a loyal and religious Anglican. He seemed to lament very much that, by the means of irregular and indiscreet preaching, the generality of the nation were possessed with such dangerous mistakes as to think 'they might be religious first, and then just and merciful; that they might sell their consciences, and yet have something left that was worth keeping: that they might be sure they were elected, though their lives were visibly scandalous: that to be cunning was to be wise, that to be rich was to be happy, though it is evidently false: that to speak evil of government, and to be busy in things they understood not, was no sin.' He attributed these mischiefs to "the unhappy Covenant," which had induced a state of ecclesiastical anarchy. His remedy does not strike one as worthy of so famous a divine. "He then said to me 'that the way to restore this nation to a more meek and Christian temper was to have the body of divinity (or so much of it as was needful to be known by the common people) to be put into fifty-two homilies, or sermons, of such a length as not to exceed a third or fourth part of an hour's reading: and these needful points to be made so clear and plain, that those of a mean capacity might know what was necessary to be believed, and what God requires to be done: and then some plain applications of trial and conviction: and these to be read every Sunday in the year, as infallibly as the blood circulates the body at a set time; and then as certainly begun again, and continued the year following." This somewhat "grandmotherly" scheme commended itself at a later period to the excellent TILLOTSON, who actually went some way, in conjunction with PATRICK and BURNET, to put it into execution. But, indeed, the day for homilies set forth by authority had long passed by: and politicians, ecclesiastical not less than civil, would have to make their count with the demands of a nation which had for ever left the disciplinary methods of the præ-Revolutionary period. The past and the future of the English Commonwealth were parted by a stream of blood, and nothing could ever again obliterate that barrier.

A contemporary of Sanderson, who afterwards sat also in the bishop's seat at Lincoln, the acute and learned, but timorous and time-serving, THOMAS BARLOW (1607–1691) related to Walton, in a letter which is appended to Sanderson's Life, the answer that Sanderson returned to "a person of quality" who had privately asked him "what course a young divine should take in his studies to enable him to be a good casuist." "His answer was, that a convenient understanding of the learned languages (at least of Hebrew, Greek, and Latin) and a sufficient knowledge of arts and sciences presupposed, there were two things in human literature, a comprehension of which would be of very great use to enable a man to be a rational and able casuist, which otherwise was very difficult, if not impossible. (1) A convenient knowledge of moral philosophy; especially that part of it which treats of the nature of human actions. . . . For every case of conscience being only this—Is this action good or bad? May I do it, or may I not? He who (in these) knows not how and whence human actions become morally good and evil never can (in hypothesi) rationally and certainly determine whether this or that particular action be so. (2) A convenient knowledge of the nature and obligation of laws in general . . . for every case of conscience being only this—Is this lawful for me, or is it not? and the law the only rule and measure by which I must judge of the lawfulness or unlawfulness of any action; it evidently follows that he who (in these) knows not the nature and obligation of laws, never can be a good casuist, or rationally assure himself (or others) of the lawfulness or unlawfulness of actions in particular." The comparative simplicity of casuistic method described in these words is characteristic of the English casuists. They were not, as was the case with their Roman contemporaries, confused by the mass of conflicting authorities, or by the radically false classification of sins as mortal and venial, or by the theory of probabilism, or by the requirements of the confessional, or by the perverse logic of the cloister. They dealt with genuine questions, actually proposed to them, and these they answered by applying with the broad reasonableness of sincere and sensible men certain fundamental principles of morality which assumed and received the assent of the conscience. In trying to estimate the part which the English casuists played in the national life in the seventeenth century, we must bear in mind that the relative importance of the clergy in that age was immensely greater than is now the case. Puritanism in its own way magnified the ministry hardly less than the opposed system of Laudianism; it was not until the rise of the sects, and especially of the Quakers, that English people grew familiar with the notion of a Christianity which ignored the ministry. The constitutional position of the English clergy was far stronger then than now, and their personal weight was infinitely greater. Literature, science, and politics still remained to a large extent within the clerical profession, or subject to clerical influence. The pulpit was a powerful engine of influence, and the press was normally controlled by the Bench. It did not seem extravagant, then, to lay on the clergy the task of moral guidance; their office still carried authority,[1] and men turned instinctively to them for advice and direction. But the casuists of the modern age are not divines, but dramatists and novel-writers, who dictate to the semi-educated classes their moral standards by subtly re-issuing to them their prejudices. Whether the new casuistry is an improvement on the old remains yet undecided.

---

[1] *cf.* Mr. Charles Booth's statement: "The clergy and ministers have no authority that is recognised, but their professional character remains, and owing to it they perhaps lose influence."—*Life and Labour in London*, third series, vol. vii. p. 428.

Toleration

I

IT is one of the ironies of history that France, the country in which religious bigotry found its extremest expression, led the way in adopting a policy of toleration. As early as 1598, the Edict of Nantes secured to the Protestant minority in that country rights which were still refused to English Nonconformists nearly a century later. When Richelieu finally crushed the political power of the Huguenots, he maintained intact the religious settlement. Dr. Gardiner discusses the reason why England, where, as he freely admits, "the condition of mutual forbearance which renders toleration possible"[1] was more nearly approached than elsewhere, yet lagged behind France in adopting the policy. "Mutual forbearance" is, indeed, the condition of genuine and lasting toleration, but the political and ecclesiastical situation in England was very unfavourable to an adoption of that policy. "It is not to be denied,"

---

[1] *History of England*, 1603-42, vol. vii. p. 159.

says Dr. Gardiner, "that the adoption of a system of toleration would have been in some respects attended with greater difficulties in England than it was in France. What was granted in France was a local toleration for those who lived in certain places. Nothing of the kind would meet the requirements of England. Toleration there must be not local but universal. The men who reverenced the communion-table as an altar, and the men who looked upon it as a mere table to which no reverence was due, lived side by side in the same street." We may observe that this necessity of universal toleration in England delayed the victory of reason until the policy of toleration had been deliberately and intelligently adopted by the nation, and thus secured its permanence. French toleration was the creature of Richelieu's profound statecraft; it had no guarantees in the reason and conscience of the French people, who acquiesced readily enough in its repudiation by the fanaticism of Louis XIV. less than a century after its estabment. Dr. Gardiner continues: "The main condition of toleration was the absence of fear lest toleration should be used as a means of attack upon those who granted it. The discovery that the dominant religion in France was in no danger from the assaults of the Huguenots had made toleration possible there. Laud had no such comforting assurance in England. As the leader of a governing minority, he was beset with fear that his work would crumble away the moment the strong hand of Government was withdrawn from its support. All the more tolerant maxims with which he had started were stripped away from him by the falseness of his position. In proportion as his weakness grew more evident his intolerance increased. The true word and thought could not proceed from one who was occupying the ground on which he was standing. Not till a Government arose whose ecclesiastical institutions rested on the conviction of the nation, and which could therefore afford to deal generously with the few who held divergent opinions, would the doctrine of toleration take its place among the accepted principles of English politics."[1]

Dr. Gardiner, in this luminous and characteristic paragraph, omits a circumstance of some importance. Toleration can never really commend itself to men who believe themselves possessed of a divinely-ordained system. It is unquestionably true that Laud was "the leader of a governing minority," and that the inherent falseness of his position compelled him to maintain himself in power by a "reign of terror," but it is equally certain that such was not his view of the situation.

[1] *Ibid.*, vol. viii. pp. 165-6.

His intolerance had its origin, not in political exigency, though this contributed arguments of its own in support, but in religious conviction. In this respect, indeed, the archbishop and his enemies stood on the same ground. The fiercest opponents of toleration in the England of that age were the Presbyterians, who believed their system of church order to be divinely instituted, and their intolerance, also, became more vehement as their political position grew more insecure. The nation, as a whole, believed as little in the Episcopalianism of Laud as in the Presbyterianism of the Westminster Assembly; both these successive fanaticisms had behind them eager and enthusiastic minorities, but neither could hold its own against the decisive repugnance of the general sentiment which both in turn provoked. The general sentiment, however, was slow to make itself felt, and there were reasons why toleration seemed less rational than it was finally confessed to be. We may add to Dr. Gardiner's explanation of English intolerance two other circumstances. English Nonconformity was not merely diffused, but it was also various. The spectacle of the sects was neither edifying nor attractive. Non-Anglican Christianity presented an aspect of unreason and anarchy, which scared from the project of religious toleration those sober-minded and equitable Englishmen who would naturally have been the first to embrace it. Moreover, this anarchic and irrational sectarianism was passionately aggressive and anti-episcopal. We may, and indeed we ought to, make allowance for the madness which oppression never fails to cause, but we cannot ignore the excuse for intolerance which was provided by the insane violence of the sectaries. They spoke with two voices. With the one they pleaded reasonably, sometimes eloquently, for liberty of conscience and worship; with the other they called for the destruction of the English hierarchy, upon which they poured forth the most venomous insults. The intense hatred of the English bishops, which is the common and most prominent feature of sectarian literature, is not altogether easy to explain. Something, perhaps, must be allowed for the fact that in England there was no such consciousness of the inherent Divineness of the Church as existed in Roman Catholic countries. The whole disciplinary system, which then extended over a far larger range of human action, and affected a more considerable proportion of the people than now, bore upon men as the action of the individual bishops, who often reluctantly had to administer it. As a matter of fact, the idiosyncrasy of the bishop, or his personal beliefs, did count for much in his diocesan government. Puritans were harried in one diocese, caressed in another. Bishop WILLIAMS in Lincoln was ordering the communion table to be brought into the body of the church, while Archbishop LAUD in Canterbury was vigorously insisting on its position and inclosure at the east end. The *Book of Sports* was ignored in Exeter and enforced in Winchester. It was impossible to recognise the impersonal law of the Church through the bewildering varieties of episcopal practice. In taking this personal aspect the episcopal administration lost the semblance of equity, and was resented as a capricious tyranny. Thus experience seemed to give countenance to the anti-episcopal prejudice, which was extremely strong throughout the Protestant world. We have shown in an earlier lecture how unpopular the bishops had become within England itself when the Long Parliament began its sessions; outside of England, within the Protestant world, bishops were not found, and this suggestive fact was forced on English attention at that juncture precisely at which the principles of Protestantism were directly endangered by the flood-tide of counter-Reformation. However the bitter dislike of the bishops may be explained, the fact on which we have commented is certain, viz. that the violent anti-Episcopalianism of the sectaries hindered the advent of the toleration for which they clamoured by seeming to demonstrate that such toleration was inconsistent with the security of Church and State.

II

Among the leaders of the movement of thought which finally established religious toleration as one of the axioms of English politics must be named the garrulous and pedantic, but shrewd and broadminded JAMES I. His curious homilies to Parliament constantly dealt with the nature, measure, and object of religious coercion, for, both as a polemical theologian and as a statesman, he was continually required to explain and justify the oppressive proceedings of the English State with regard to recusant Papists and rebellious sectaries. The sectarian pamphleteers, who now began to press for toleration, were naturally eager to commend their arguments by the authority of the Sovereign, in whose name and, in some sense, in whose interest they were oppressed; and as a matter of fact, quotations from the king's speeches are plentifully scattered over the tracts of the period. The writers appeal from the bishops to the king, and invoke the king against the bishops. For obvious reasons it served their turn to exempt the sovereign from their criticisms of the Government, and to direct their whole strength against the hierarchy.

The protagonists of religious liberty in this country were members of the most suspected and oppressed of all the sects—Anabaptists as their opponents called them, Baptists as they preferred to call themselves. In or about the year 1611 Thomas Helwys arrived in England from Amsterdam, where he was known as the pastor of the Baptist church founded by the erratic John Smyth, commonly called the Se-baptist, because, unable to accord with any existing church, he publicly baptised himself. Helwys gathered a congregation in London, which is reckoned as the first general Baptist Church established in England. From this congregation there proceeded a series of bold and able pleas for religious liberty. We may select as an excellent example of this literature a substantial pamphlet published anonymously by a member of Helwys's Church in 1615. The title is worth reproducing in full :—[1]

"*Objections answered by way of dialogue, wherein is proved by the Law of God: by the Law of our Land: and by his Majesty's many testimonies that no man ought to be persecuted for his religion, so he testify*

---

[1] *v. Tracts on Liberty of Conscience and Persecution, 1614–1661, edited for the Hanserd Knollys Society, with an historical introduction by Edward Bean Underhill*, p. 85. [London, 1846.]

his allegiance by the Oath appointed by law." The pamphlet is prefaced by an epistle subscribed " by Christ's unworthy Witnesses, His Majesty's faithful subjects : commonly (but most falsely) called Anabaptists." In this epistle they disclaim the anarchic sentiments with which the Anabaptists were commonly credited, and which unquestionably weighed most with the public mind when the policy of toleration was debated. "We do unfeignedly acknowledge the authority of earthly magistrates, God's blessed ordinance, and that all earthly authority and command appertains unto them ; let them command what they will, we must obey, either to do or suffer upon pain of God's displeasure, besides their punishment : but all men must let God alone with His right, which is to be lord and lawgiver to the soul, and not command obedience for God where He commandeth none. And this is only that which we dare not but maintain upon the peril of our souls, which is greater than bodily affliction. And only for the maintenance of Christ's right herein, do false prophets and deceivers (who by that craft are clothed in fine apparel, and fare deliciously every day) labour to make us odious in the ears and eyes of prince and people, knowing well that if they had not power by persecution to force men to dissemble to believe as they, their kingdom and gain would soon come to nought."[1] This is an instructive introduction to an appeal for liberty of conscience, for it breathes the arrogant spirit of persecution. So long as the dissentient minority held the majority to be "false prophets and deceivers," it is no marvel that the majority doubted the practical wisdom of conceding toleration. The pamphlet is well represented by the introduction. It is cast into the form of a dialogue between an "Anti-Christian" and a "Christian," with an "Indifferent Man" intervening, and passing by easy stages from umpire to convert. The objection that such liberty as was demanded could not be granted without danger to the State is well stated and answered.

> "*A.* If it were as you would have it, that all religions should be suffered, how dangerous would it be to the king's person and state! What treacheries and treasons would be plotted!
>
> "*I.* Indeed that is a thing greatly to be suspected, but if permission of all religions should be cleared of that, there is no question but it might prevail with the king and state.
>
> "*C.* If it be not cleared of that, then let all men abhor it."[2]

It is remarkable that the author is prepared to extend toleration even to the Papists.

---
[1] *Ibid.*, p. 100.   [2] *Ibid.*, pp. 113-14.

"And for the Papists," he says, "may it not justly be suspected that one chief cause of all their treasons hath been because of all the compulsions that have been used against their consciences, in compelling them to the worship practised in public, according to the law of this land; which, being taken away, there is no doubt but they would be much more peaceable; as we see it verified in divers other nations where no such compulsion is used, for if they might have freedom in their religion unto their faithful allegiance to the king, the fear of the king's laws, and their own prosperity and peace, would make them live more inoffensively in that respect."

Such sentiments as these, within ten years of the Gunpowder Plot, are certainly surprising, and the reference to foreign countries as the homes of religious liberty is suggestive.

The familiar parallel between the kings of Israel and Christian sovereigns, which had been the very keystone of Anglicanism, and, indeed, by the Canons of 1603 had been raised to an article of faith, is boldly examined and repudiated. There is some historic interest in the author's account of the apprehension with which the advent of James, from Presbyterian Scotland, had been, in the first instance, regarded by English Churchmen.

"*I.* The convocation of bishops, and the rest have made a canon, that whosoever shall affirm that the king's majesty hath not the same power in causes ecclesiastical, under the gospel that the godly kings of Israel had under the law, let him be excommunicate, *ipso facto*.

"*C.* Yes, they have so. In the beginning of his Majesty's reign, when they had got him sure unto them—of the which they so much doubted, as with my own ears I heard some of their chief followers say, when his highness was coming into England, 'Now must steeples down, and we shall have no more high commission!' (with lamentation they spake it)—then they made this canon; because their consciences are convinced that they stand only by his power; and if his hand be turned, their spiritual power of darkness falleth to the pit of darkness, from whence it came."[1]

The writer is at his best when he argues that hypocritical conformity, which is all that persecution can secure, gives no real security for true allegiance. "If I should come to church,

---

[1] *v. Ibid.*, pp. 130-1.

and not of conscience, but for other respects, as many Papists and other hypocrites do, to God it were most abominable, and what faithfulness can be hoped for in such towards his Majesty's person and state? Can any godly, wise man think that he that playeth the dissembling hypocrite with God, that he will do less with men, and will not work any villainy, if it were in his power? And, therefore, herein you compelling me by tyranny, to bring my body whereunto my spirit cannot be brought, you compel me to hypocrisy with God and man; for if my heart were not faithful in sincerity to his Majesty's crown and dignity, as I take God to witness (before whom I must be condemned or justified) it is, these courses would rather harden my heart to work villainy than otherwise."[1]

When we read such sane and persuasive reasoning, we wonder that it failed so completely to carry conviction; but the reason is discovered when we read on to the end. The last half of the pamphlet destroys the impression made by the first. The author lays aside his engaging moderation in order to give rein to the frenzied hatred of the bishops which is consuming him. He proves to the "Indifferent Man" that the Roman Church is the Apocalyptic beast, and

---

[1] *v. Ibid.*, p. 139.

the Church of England the beast's image, and that all the seer's curses are properly due to conformity. "The sum of all which is, that whosoever openly professeth obedience and subjection to that spiritual cruel power of Rome, the beast, or to that spiritual cruel power of England, his image (wheresoever they, or either of them, are exalted), such a one, and such persons, shall drink of the wine of God's wrath, and be tormented in fire and brimstone, and shall have no rest day nor night for evermore."[1] The "Indifferent Man" suggests that, when all is said, "they have the word and sacraments in the English assemblies," and that "it cannot be denied but that the ministers preach many excellent truths, and do bring people to much reformation in many things"; but he is at once assured that these semblances of piety are only the transforming robe of Satan.

"So his ministers, if they should teach all lies, men would not be deceived by them, nor plead for them, but because they teach many truths, people receive them." Moreover, their alleged reformation does not really amount to much, for it only affects men's morals and leaves them ignorant of religion, content to submit to "anti-Christ's abominations." The writer is thorough-going;

---

[1] *v. Ibid.*, p. 147.

he will admit no compromise; he quotes and adopts the opinion of another sectary, "that there is nothing to be expected from Christ by any member of the Church of England, but a pouring out of his eternal wrath upon them."[1]

The pamphlet concludes with an earnest argument against the common practice of the sectaries when persecuted of flying from the country. The sectarian literature of the time is very fairly represented by the piece we have examined. Broad truths are there, which in course of time will receive universal recognition and become the axioms of civilised society; but they are embedded in the crudest fanaticism, which now moves contemptuous wonder, but then stirred genuine alarm. The fanaticism of the context arrested more notice than the truth of the text itself, and added to the normal distaste of new notions a distinctive objection, intelligible to the simplest, and capable of effective statement in the hands of the skilled controversialist. Such a controversialist was the famous BISHOP HALL, whose *Common Apology against the Brownists*, published originally in 1610, and several times republished in the course of the century, may stand as an excellent example of the Anglican apologetic. We may say of this literature the

---
[1] *v. Ibid.*, p. 156.

precise opposite of what was said above. The central thesis is unsound, but it is presented in a context so reasonable and attractive that the unsoundness escapes notice. Hall definitely affirms the rightfulness of coercion in the matter of religion.

"Your subtle doctor," he says, "can tell us from Bernard, that 'Faith is to be persuaded, not to be compelled'; yet, let him remember that the guests must be compelled to come in, though not to eat when they are come: compelled, not by persuasions, for these were the first invitations, therefore by further means."[1] And, again, he refers with approbation to "Augustin's resolution concerning the sharp penalties imposed upon the Donatists, in his time, with his excellent defences of those proceedings." There is a suggestion of violence in his reference to that plea of conscience which was commonly on sectarian lips. "Conscience is a common plea even to those you hate: we inquire not how strong it is, but how well informed; not whether it suggests this, but whereupon. To go against the conscience is sin; to follow a misinformed conscience is sin also; if you do not the first, we know you are faulty in the second. He that is greater than the conscience will not take this for an excuse."[2]

---

[1] *v. Works*, ed. Wynter, vol. ix. p. 21. [Oxford, 1863.]
[2] *v. Ibid.*, p. 37.

Of course Hall, as a sound Anglican, builds much on the precedents of the Old Testament, while he denounces the certainly not more irrational literalism of the sectaries with respect to the New. The denunciations of Episcopacy, in which his opponents indulged, he meets by adducing proofs of the friendly attitude of the foreign Churches towards the Church of England.

"I reverence from my soul (so doth our Church, their dear sister) those worthy foreign churches which have chosen and followed those forms of outward government that are every way fittest for their own condition. It is enough for your sect to censure them. I touch nothing common to them with you."[1]

"I blush to see so wilful a slander fall from the pen of a Christian, that all reformed churches renounce our prelacy as anti-christian? Yea, what one foreign divine of note hath not given to our clergy the right hand of fellowship?

"These sisters have learned to differ, and yet to love and reverence each other: and in these cases to enjoy their own forms without prescription of necessity or censure."[2] It was, of course, only the divine-right, exclusive Episcopacy of Laudianism which was intolerable to the reformed Churches, but in 1610 that was not maintained by the leading

---

[1] v. *Ibid.*, p. 40. [2] v. *Ibid.*, p. 61.

representatives of the Church of England. In this pamphlet Hall justifies the Anglican ministry on other grounds than that of "apostolic succession," grounds that would equally justify episcopal and non-episcopal ministries. "Call them what you please, superintendents, that is, bishops, prelates, priests, lecturers, parsons, vicars, etc., if they preach Christ truly, upon true inward abilities, upon a sufficient if not perfect outward vocation; such a one (let all histories witness) for the substance, as hath been ever in the Church since the apostles' times; they are pastors and doctors allowed by Christ. We stand not upon circumstances and appendances of the fashions of ordination, manner of choice, attire, titles, maintenance: but if, for substance, these be not true pastors and doctors, Christ had never any in his Church since the apostles left the earth."[1]

Nothing could be more commendably reasonable, and as the writer takes up the sectarian contentions one by one and exposes their grotesque extravagance, the reader receives an overwhelming impression of intractable and irrational fanaticism encountered by sane and balanced reasoning. Hall points with crushing effect to the dissidence of dissent displayed in "the English-parlour-full at Amsterdam." "Our land," he says, "you could like

[1] *v. Ibid.*, p. 54.

it well, if you might be lords alone. Thanks be to God it likes not you: and justly thinks the meanest corner too good for so mutinous a generation. When it is weary of peace, it will recall you. You, that neither in prison, nor on the seas, nor in the coasts of Virginia, nor in your way, nor in Netherland, could live in peace: what shall we hope of your case at home?"[1] "Will you never leave," he asks scornfully, "till you have wrangled yourselves out of the world?" He exults in the controversial triumphs won by Anglicans in the chronic contest with Rome. Their "learned pens," he says, "have pulled down more of the walls of Rome than all the corner-creeping Brownists in the world shall ever be able to do while Amsterdam standeth."[2] As we read the effective denunciations of the sectaries we ought to remember that the writers were entrenched in privilege and power, while their opponents were deprived even of liberty. In spite of their amazing fanaticism the sectaries had got hold of the sound principle; in spite of their attractive reasonableness the Anglicans were enslaved by the false.

---

[1] *v. Ibid.*, p. 102. [2] *v. Ibid.*, p. 113.

III

The Laudian policy of uniformity, secured by using the royal prerogative unflinchingly in the interest of divine-right Episcopalianism, permitted no place to religious sectaries. Toleration was dismissed as politically unsafe and morally wrong. Nonconformists were, in James I.'s notable phrase, "harried" out of the kingdom. Even the congregations of foreign Protestants were not permitted to remain outside the national system of religion. Laud could not run the risk of having an object-lesson in non-episcopalian Christianity offered to English Churchmen within England itself. "The edifice which he was rearing was of so artificial a character that he dared not withdraw his eye from it for an instant."[1] The immigrants were to be permitted the use of their native language, but they must employ a translation of the English Prayer-book, and their children born in England must attend the parish churches. An appeal to the king secured release from the order to use the Prayer-book, but the more substantial grievance implied in the treatment of their English-born children was insisted upon.[2] In the

---

[1] Gardiner, *History of England*, 1603–1642, vol. viii. p. 120.

[2] This proceeding was charged against the archbishop at his trial as showing that he had "traitorously endeavoured to cause

accounts of his province made to the king during the seven years from 1633 to 1639 we have a curious revelation of Laud's mind and of the religious state of England as he saw it. Reading between the lines, it is plain enough that he was dimly conscious of failure. The sectaries—"Brownists and other separatists," "Anabaptists," and the like—were not yielding to his treatment. Patience and threatening were equally without effect, and he had come to think that the only adequate method would be to expel them from the country—a method which was a patent confession of failure. In his latest account—that for the year 1639—he writes despondently of his own diocese: "The great thing which is amiss there, and beyond my power to remedy, is the stiffness of divers Anabaptists and separatists from the Church of England, especially in and about the

---

division and discord between the Church of England and other reformed Churches." Laud justified himself by pleading that the example of the foreign Protestants "standing so strictly to their own discipline wrought upon the party in England which were addicted to them, and made them more averse than otherwise they would have been to the present government of the Church of England." He urged the political danger of tolerating such an "imperium in imperio," and characteristically quoted Exodus xii. 49 : "Our law shall be to him that is homeborn, and to the stranger that sojourns among you."

γ. *Works*, vol. iii. pp. 421, 422. [Library of Anglo-Catholic Theology.]

parts near Ashford. And I do not find either by my own experience, or by any advice from my officers, that this is like to be remedied, unless the statute concerning abjuration of your kingdom, or some other way by the power of the temporal law or state be thought upon. But how fit that may be to be done for the present, especially in these broken times, I humbly submit to your majesty's wisdom, having often complained of this before." In the diocese of Hereford he reports that the Brownists were particularly active, "and when they hear of any inquiry made after them, they slip out into another diocese." "However," he concludes dejectedly, "your majesty may hereby see how these schisms increase in all parts of your dominions."[1] The notion of leaving the country as the only solution of the problem of conscientious refusal to obey the law was already familiar to the English Puritans. As early as 1620 the *Mayflower* had sailed on that voyage to New England which later generations of Englishmen would

---

[1] The accounts are printed in vol. v. of Laud's *Works* in the Library of Anglo-Catholic Theology (see especially pp. 326, 336, 347, 355, 361). Laud describes the sectaries as "all of the poorer sort, and very simple," "very busy, miserable, poor." Their leaders—Brewer, Fenner, and Turner—had been imprisoned and banished, but apparently had returned. Brewer was recaptured "and was called before the high commission, where he stood silent, but in such a jeering, scornful manner, as I scarce ever saw the like."

regard as a memorable turning-point in the history of their race.

The departure of the pilgrims is said to have given occasion to a remarkable speech by JOHN ROBINSON, "the father of the Independents," which merits reproduction in any history of toleration.

"Brethren," he said, "we are now quickly to part from one another, and whether I may ever live to see your face on earth any more, the God of heaven only knows; but whether the Lord has appointed that or no, I charge you before God and His blessed angels, that you follow me no farther than you have seen me follow the Lord Jesus Christ. If God reveal anything to you, by any other instrument of His, be as ready to receive it as ever you were to receive any truth by my ministry: for I am verily persuaded, the Lord has more truth yet to break forth out of His holy word. For my part, I cannot sufficiently bewail the condition of the reformed churches, who are come to a period in religion, and will go at present no farther than the instruments of their Reformation. The Lutherans cannot be drawn to go beyond what Luther saw: whatever part of His will our God has revealed to Calvin, they will rather die than embrace it: and the Calvinists, you see, stick fast where they were left by that great man of God, who yet saw not all things. This is a misery much to be lamented, for though they were burning and shining lights in their times, yet they penetrated not into the whole counsel of God, but were they now living, would be as willing to embrace farther light as that which they first received. I beseech you remember, it is an article of your church-covenant, that you be ready to receive whatever truth shall be made known to you from the written word of God. Remember that, and every other article of your sacred covenant. But I must here withal exhort you to take heed what you receive as truth—examine it, consider it, and compare it with other scriptures of truth, before you receive it, for it is not possible the Christian world should come so lately out of such thick anti-christian darkness, and that perfection of knowledge should break forth at once. I must also advise you to abandon, avoid, and shake off the name of Brownists: it is a mere nickname, and a brand for the making religion and the professors of it odious to the Christian world."[1]

This dignified and courageous language was far beyond the comprehension of the Pilgrim

---

[1] *v.* Neal's *History of the Puritans*, vol. i. p. 476. [London, 1837.]

Fathers, and, indeed, probably gives an exaggerated impression of its author's tolerance; for though spoken in 1620, the earliest extant report of the speech belongs to the year 1646, when the bigotry of the Independents had provoked general protests, and there was a desire to demonstrate the liberality of Independent tenets. The address, as we have it, "owes something to the reporter's controversial needs."[1] Still, when all allowances have been made, Robinson's speech remains a notable utterance, and marks a stage in the evolution of religious liberty. It goes far beyond the position maintained in the most famous of all the pleadings for theological tolerance which the seventeenth century has bequeathed to us—Jeremy Taylor's *Liberty of Prophesying*, published in 1647.

At Amsterdam and Leyden were numerous colonies of religious exiles, to which, as the policy of uniformity was more rigorously pressed in England, recruits continually arrived. Laud perceived new risks arising from these centres of untamable sectarianism. Commerce and politics were ever carrying abroad English citizens

---

[1] The literary history of this famous address is given shortly in the *Dictionary of National Biography*, vol. xlix. p. 21. For the purposes of a history of toleration the personal question is of little importance. As a document of 1646 it may even be thought more astonishing than as an oration of 1620.

in pursuit of gain or in the king's service. Were they to be corrupted in their absence from the national fold, and to bring back with them the very heresies which, with such labour and difficulty, had been removed from the State? With characteristic energy the archbishop forced the Prayer-book on the merchant colonies and on the English regiments serving abroad; he even attempted to stretch across the Atlantic and extend religious conformity to the Puritan communities which were taking root in America, but in this direction his power was too inadequate to his designs, and the determined attitude of the colonists threatened the total loss of their allegiance, if here also it were to be made the pretext for oppressing their conscience. The sudden and complete collapse of the Laudian system before the uprising of the Puritan sentiment of the nation seemed at first to promise an epoch of religious liberty based on a substantial religious agreement; but this promise failed of fulfilment mainly for two reasons. On the one hand, as we have already pointed out, the Presbyterian system was intensely hostile to the principle of toleration; on the other hand, toleration was quickly discredited by the astonishing outbreak of fanaticism which was induced by the mental and moral strain of the civil war following upon the destruction, amid general contumely, of the ecclesiastical system of the country. It will, perhaps, be worth while to examine these more closely.

IV

The Presbyterian system was a divine-right system, as were the rival systems—Roman, Anglican, and even Congregational—and as such it was exclusive and intolerant; but its intolerance took a more vehement and conscientious character from the circumstances under which it had taken shape. To begin with, it was a very new system; to its adherents it had the aspect of a divine revelation. Then it professed to base itself utterly on the Scriptures, and as these were in the hands of all its members, it was a thoroughly intelligible system, which carried its divine credentials on its front. It was, moreover, a strictly logical system; it left no place anywhere for anything else; and being severely biblical, at a time when the Old Testament was generally accepted as hardly less authoritative than the New, it was properly a territorial system, covering the whole area, and requiring within its dominion the eviction or destruction of every rival. Being thus scriptural, logical, and territorial, it commended itself to all Puritanically minded laymen as the most satisfactory of all known substitutes for the ancient, and now abhorrent, Church of Rome. It allowed no goodness in and sought no connection with the mystic Babylon, and while thus satisfying to the full the rancour of Protestantism, it was as intolerant of anarchy as Rome itself. Presbyterianism implied an ordering of the State not less than an ordering of the Church.

Perhaps no better evidence as to the spirit of Presbyterianism can be found than that provided in the sermons of the period; and of this evidence it needs no saying that we possess abundance. The Long Parliament early in its course adopted as a regular institution the monthly Fast, which the House of Commons observed by attending two or three sermons in St. Margaret's, Westminster, preached by divines specially nominated by the House, which regularly thanked them afterwards and requested them to publish their sermons. The House of Lords similarly appointed fasts, attended sermons in Westminster Abbey, and regularly thanked the preachers and authorised the publication of their discourses.

These parliamentary sermons form a body of contemporary literature of no mean historic value.

In them are reflected the very emotions of the time, and they reveal its inner mind. In the pulpit the preachers, almost always members of the Westminster Assembly, were able to say what they thought without the disabling consciousness that Selden was revolving some bitter and humbling sarcasm, or that the "Dissenting Brethren" were eager to turn on them that biblical artillery which they accounted peculiarly their own.

The sermons may be gathered under three heads, marking successive political stages. At first they are mainly concerned with pulling down the whole Laudian system, with its Romish affinities and temper of dangerous compromise. Then, under the influence of Scotland, they are directed to the defence, exaltation, and enforcement of "The Solemn League and Covenant." Finally, when the power of the sectaries has become everywhere manifest, they thunder against Toleration. An excellent example of these parliamentary sermons is the discourse preached before the Lords in Westminster Abbey by WILLIAM JENKYNS, "Minister of God's Word at Christ Church, London," a prominent defender of Presbyterianism, on the 25th of February, 1645. The sermon fills thirty-six closely printed pages, and on a reasonable estimate must have taken two hours to deliver, if the preacher actually spoke all that he published. In his peroration he takes a sentence from the description of Ezekiel's vision—" the spirit of the living creature was in the wheels "—and uses it with much skill and effect. The spirit of " carnal interest," he says, has been, and still is, the mainspring of parliamentary action, and against it he thunders. The following is a curiously just estimate of the course of events :—

" Our reformation, in the destructive part of it to Episcopacy and scandalous ministers, was prosecuted with much eagerness; spectators rejoiced to see our zeal for the Lord, in putting down them with their crosses, images, and crucifixes, but did not this wheel move also according to the spirit of carnal interest? were not the men and their usurped power, lately very burdensome and prejudicial to us, to our estates and liberties, not to say to our honours and rule? and was not the ejection of those, who knew how to fish for tithes, though not for souls, a very taking plausible thing? interest agreed with it: (and the breaking down of images did not bite) but when interest makes a stop, our reformation stops also : we throw down the superstitious priests and their altars, with their many idolatrous reliques, but doth our reformation proceed to deal with Jeroboam's calves too? to prohibit effectually the divulging and scattering of all those many blasphemous opinions, which are not only cried up in Dan and Bethel, but are scattered up and down from Dan to Beersheba, from one end of the kingdom to the other? Are not the second and third persons in Trinity, as much dishonoured by blotting them out of our faith, as by picturing them in a window?"

"Our care and love in encouraging the godly and painful Ministers of the Gospel was heretofore very common, and full out as commendable as common; a faithful minister that stood out under the time of Episcopal tyranny, by opposing himself to the innovations thereof, was a man of desires in the beginning of these wars; this wheel went on very nimbly too, but was there not a living creature of carnal policy that moved with it? was not respecting of godly ministers the way to be honoured before the people? and were not they the men that were fittest to move to contributions, and improve their power for exhorting to assist in the cause of late so much endangered? But when they could do no more, and by the goodness of God other means were found out for relieving of us; in a word, when interest made a stop, our love to ministers was soon at a stand, nay, declined; witness not only the disgraceful and reproachful language which every uncontrolled sectary hath inured his tongue and pen to cast upon them, but the denial of necessary subsistence to themselves and theirs, in many places where those who have wept and prayed and preached down Anti-Christ, are now accounted the only Antichristian burdens."[1] A few months later in the same place, MR. FRANCIS TAYLOR, "Pastor of Yalding in Kent, and a member of the Assembly of Divines," called for the suppression of the sectaries, whose number and audacity daily increased. "Why," he demands of the Peers, "suffer ye books to be printed under colour of maintaining liberty of conscience for the toleration of all sorts of heresies and blasphemous religions?"[2] Another preacher, MR. THOMAS HORTON, denounced as the very climax of national guilt "that sin of Libertinism and Toleration which is the ringleader to all the rest, and involves all others in it." "What?" he cried, "when we have so much appeared against Popery and Superstition, shall we now begin to think of indifferency and toleration? Certainly, it's but a sorry exchange of a bad religion for none. Although indeed it will be

---

[1] *Reformation's Remora, or Temporizing the stop of building the Temple. A Sermon*, etc., pp. 33, 34. London, 1646.

[2] *The Danger of Vows neglected and the necessity of Reformation. A Sermon*, etc., preached in the Abbey Church at Westminster, *May* 27th, 1646, p. 26. London, 1646.

PARLIAMENTARY SERMONS 243

no exchange, but rather a further confirmation; toleration of all other errors does but strengthen popery amongst the rest; which will at least think so well of itself, as to come in for a child's part."[1] Four weeks later MR. WILLIAM JENKYN again preached a passionate sermon, which was published under the title, *A sleeping Sickness the distemper of the Times, as it was discovered in its Curse and Cure.* In an epistle dedicatory he declared that the Church was wounded by "the soul-stroying opinions of Antinomians, Arminians, Anabaptists, Seekers, Anti-Scripturists, Anti-Trinitarians," and all these errors "had been more propagated these four years of Church Anarchy than in fourscore of Church Tyranny." But all was to no purpose. In this very discourse the preacher confesses the futility of exhortation. "For the Parliament," he said bitterly, "'tis a common observation that it is sermon-proof."[2] The sermons to the House of Commons in

---

[1] *Sin's discovery and Revenge, as it was delivered in a Sermon, etc., in the Abbey Church at Westminster, on Wednesday, Dec.* 30, 1646, pp. 37, 38. London, 1646.

[2] Jenkyn preached this sermon on January 27th, 1647. Students of manners will note the curious denunciation of current fashions. He enumerates scornfully the "elfish attire, shameful and yet shameless nakedness of necks and backs, those sin-black, hell-black, beauty-spots (people would not account it a beauty to be born with them), that swaggering profanation of Sabbath, drinking and riotousness among us."

S. Margaret's were of the same uncompromising character, and, as being addressed to the really dominant power in the country, even more important. All justify the contention, which indeed cannot be reasonably denied, that "as a body, the Presbyterians of 1644 and subsequent years were absolute Anti-Tolerationists." Two causes co-operated in holding them to this unfortunate position—their theory of the Church and their horror of the sectaries. The one did not admit of ecclesiastical variation; the other could not endure the apparent risks of toleration. The severity of their logic was reinforced by the timidity of panic. It must indeed be allowed that they had reason for their fears. The panic-striken mind of the Presbyterians is uncovered in the famous *Gangraena* of THOMAS EDWARDS, a work equally extravagant and characteristic, which merits the study of anyone who would understand the mental standpoint of the age, and which certainly made at the time an immense impression. It appeared in 1646, when the Presbyterian influence was waning and the Solemn League and Covenant was everywhere being ignored, and it indicates the desperate rally against sectarianism which was expressed by the preachers to whom we have made reference.

V

The course of events had steadily depressed every form of established authority and brought into prominence the more relentless and thoroughgoing advocates of change. Cromwell was driven by force of circumstances to depend ever more completely on the sectaries, and the consequences might have been foreseen. The fanatical zeal, which bore down all opposition in the field of battle, was not less effective in the field of politics; the triumph of the remodelled army, in short, drew in its train the complete overthrow of the constitution. Baxter has described the state of opinion in the army when he joined it with the plucky determination to encounter sectarianism in its stronghold. "I was almost always," he says, "when I had opportunity, disputing with one or other of them: sometimes for our civil government, and sometimes for Church order and government: sometimes for infant baptism, and oft against Anti-nomianism and Arminianism and the contrary extreme. But their most frequent and vehement disputes were for liberty of conscience, as they called it; that is, that the civil magistrate had nothing to do to determine of anything in matters of religion, by constraint or restraint, but every man might not only hold but preach and do in matters of religion what he pleased; that the civil magistrate hath nothing to do but with civil things, to keep the peace, and to protect the Church's liberties."[1] Baxter disliked and distrusted Cromwell, but his evidence on matters of fact within his own knowledge may always be trusted. "All this while," he says, "though I came not near Cromwell, his designs were visible, and I saw him continually acting his part. The Lord General [Fairfax] suffered him to govern and do all, and to choose almost all the officers of the army ... so that by degrees he had headed the greatest part of the army with Anabaptists, Anti-nomians, Seekers, or Separatists at best: and all these he tied together by the point of liberty of conscience, which was the common interest in which they did unite."[2]

Cromwell himself was, perhaps, as sincerely attached to religious toleration as any sectary in the host he led to victory, but political necessity set limits to his action. Roman Catholics were

---

[1] *Autobiography*, part i. p. 53.

[2] *v. Ibid.*, p. 57. Baxter attributes to Sir Henry Vane the special advocacy of religious toleration. "The two courses in which he had most success, and spake most plainly, were his earnest plea for universal liberty of conscience, and against the magistrates intermeddling with religion, and his teaching his followers to revile the ministry, calling them ordinarily Blackcoats, Priests, and other names which then savoured of reproach; and those gentlemen that adhered to the ministry, they said, were Priest-ridden" (p. 75).

left outside every scheme of toleration; the incompatibility of their doctrines with good citizenship was the one point on which all parties were agreed; and Prelatists were necessarily also "malignants." These, therefore, were excluded from legal recognition. The Instrument of Government [1653] under which the Protectorate was established secured toleration within certain limits. It required that there should be a public profession of Christianity with full protection for those congregations which felt themselves unable to comply with the established forms, provided that they did not abuse this liberty to the civil injury of others and to the actual disturbance of the public peace on their parts, and it was distinctly added " that this liberty was not to be extended to Popery or Prelacy." [1]

The first Parliament of the Protectorate showed a tendency to recede from the position established by the Instrument. A certain reaction was, indeed, inevitable, for not only was the extravagance of the sectaries more than ever alarming, but the influence of the clergy, Presbyterian and Independent, began to reassert itself as soon as any degree of settled government had been assured. Another assembly of divines—fourteen in number [2]—was brought

---

[1] *v.* Gardiner, *Commonwealth and Protectorate*, vol. ii. p. 290.
[2] The original design was to have a numerous assembly drawn from the whole country, and more or less representative; but this was given up in favour of a committee of selected divines.

together in Jerusalem chamber to advise Parliament in matters of religion, and it fell at once to the old task of determining the "fundamentals" of Christianity.

Of this assembly Baxter was a member, but he arrived late, and found the members engaged on a long list of "fundamentals" drafted by JOHN OWEN, the famous Independent, Dean of Christ Church.[1] Baxter was averse to lengthy doctrinal statements, and proposed the "Creed, Lord's Prayer, and Decalogue" as sufficient for parliamentary purposes, but he was overruled. Thereupon he says, "I saw that there was nothing for me and others of my mind to do, but only to hinder them from doing harm and trusting in their own opinions or crude conceits, amongst our fundamentals."[2] It was

---

[1] Owen and fourteen other ministers had protested against Socinianism in 1652, and "accompanied their protest with a scheme for the settlement of outstanding ecclesiastical questions." The House responded by appointing a Committee for the Propagation of the Gospel. "Challenged to explain what they regarded as the principles of Christianity, any assault on which was to disqualify from toleration, Owen and his supporters produced no less than fifteen fundamentals, asserting amongst other things, that none who sought to discover the mind of God except by the Holy Scriptures, who denied the ordinary doctrine of the Trinity, the incarnation, justification by grace, the necessity of forsaking sin, the resurrection, or even forsook and despised the duties of God's worship, were to be allowed to propagate their opinions." *v*. Dr. Gardiner, *Commonwealth and Protectorate*, vol. ii. p. 31.

[2] *v. Autobiography*, bk. i. pp. 198, 199.

during his stay in London in order to attend the discussions in the Jerusalem chamber that Baxter was ordered to preach before the Protector. It was eminently characteristic of the most single-minded and least tactful of Puritan divines that he thought himself called upon to denounce the interference of politicians in ecclesiastical controversies.[1] In a subsequent interview with Cromwell, Baxter, according to his own account, descanted on the blessing of the old English monarchy, and apparently caused some resentment in his formidable listener. The two men were more nearly agreed in their political judgment than they knew, but they were entirely antipathetic in temper and habit of mind. Cromwell seemed to Baxter a cynical Erastian masquerading as a religious zealot; Baxter, in the eyes of Cromwell, looked the very model of a futile and loquacious bigot.

On December 7th, 1654, the Parliament passed a resolution that "the true, reformed, protestant,

---

[1] *Ibid.*, p. 205. "I knew not which way to provoke him better to his duty than by preaching on 1 Corinthians i. 10 against the divisions and distractions of the Church, and shewing how mischievous a thing it was for politicians to maintain such divisions for their own ends, that they might fish in troubled waters, and keep the Church by its divisions in a state of weakness, lest it should be able to offend them, and to shew the necessity and means of union. But the plainness and nearness I heard were displeasing to him and his courtiers, but they put it up."

Christian religion, as it is contained in the Holy Scriptures of the Old and New Testaments, and no other shall be asserted and maintained as the public profession of these nations." The question of the limits of the toleration which should be granted to the sectaries who stood outside the established system of religion was next debated; and here it speedily became apparent that the old persecuting leaven of the Covenant was working potently in the legislature. There was a victim ready to hand in the person of the irrepressible Socinian JOHN BIDDLE, who had once more brought himself within reach of the law by publishing two heretical Catechisms. It was ordered (December 13th, 1654), " that John Biddle be committed prisoner to the Gate house in Westminster: and there be kept close prisoner, without pen, ink, or paper, in order to a further proceeding against him." To what lengths of severity the Parliament would have proceeded against opinions regarded almost universally with horror does not appear, for the breach with the Protector on other grounds led soon to its dissolution, and Biddle's case passed into the more merciful hands of Cromwell himself, who, however deeply he abhorred Socinianism, was resolutely averse to severe measures of religious suppression. "If his views on toleration," says Dr. Gardiner, "did not quite reach the standard of the nineteenth century, [it must be allowed not only that]¹ they were in advance of all but the choicest spirits of the day in which he lived, but also that his practice time after time outran his profession. Again and again he had associated himself with the opinion that blasphemy and atheism, whether they were dangerous to the Government or not, were insufferable in a Christian State. Yet when he was called on to put his opinion in practice, his generosity of spirit proved too strong for the theories, and he showed himself anxious to alleviate the lot of the sufferers, if not to remit entirely the penalties imposed on them by law."² Biddle, whose aggressive courage almost forced the most tolerant of governors to approve severity, was finally banished to the Scilly Isles by an order of the Council. Socinians were exasperating enough, but they were few in number; it was otherwise with the Quakers, who made their appearance during the Commonwealth, and almost at a bound became a numerous community.

---

[1] This must be inserted to complete the sentence. For once Dr. Gardiner exhibits an example of slipshod writing. In his case, certainly, the exception proves the rule.

[2] *v. Commonwealth and Protectorate,* vol. iii. pp. 209, 210.

VI

We have said that the most resolute opposition to religious liberty came from the Presbyterians; it is important to remember that the Quaker movement was in its origin a vehement protest against the doctrine and discipline of the Solemn League and Covenant. "In the really formative years of Fox's religious development, not Episcopacy, but Presbyterianism was the dominant form of Church government. Calvin's *Institutes*, not Hooker's *Ecclesiastical Polity*, was the text-book of the clergy with whom he was brought in contact." It is no doubt true that, after the restoration, the Quakers endured at the hands of the dominant Episcopalians the bitterest persecution; but still their main and most consistent testimony was against the doctrine of the Presbyterians. "Still the Calvinistic teaching was that against which he (Fox) bore his most persistent protest, and when his young disciple Barclay gave literary and logical form to the new sect's teaching, his apology was a veiled attack upon the Westminster Confession, the great manifesto of seventeenth-century Calvinism."[1]

The Quakers in principle were the most tolerant

---

[1] *v. George Fox*, by Thomas Hodgkin, pp. 4–6. [Leaders of Religion Series.]

of religious men, and it is claimed for them that alone of all Christians they have never persecuted others; but against this honourable distinction must be advanced the fact that their tolerant principles were long obscured by their fanatical conduct, and that their characteristic extravagances threw back the cause of toleration by associating it with intolerable disorder and the most grotesque eccentricities. They shocked public decency, they insulted public order, they threatened the rights of property. "Magistrates detested them for their insolence in refusing to acknowledge the dignity of local authority by bowing or removing their hats, whilst they alienated the masses by condemning their revelries. Religious people of fixed opinions were irritated not only by the pertinacity of their arguments, but by the unseemly interruption of their favourite preachers. Behind all this was a widely-spread conviction that the doctrine of the inner light was a blasphemous assumption of the personal inspiration of the Almighty." Baxter's account of them reflects the horror they inspired in religious men, not unfriendly to the notion of a wide religious liberty. "The Quakers," he says in his autobiography, "were but the Ranters turned from horrid profaneness and blasphemy, to a life of extreme austerity on the other side. Their doctrines were mostly the same with the Ranters. They make the light which every man hath within him to be his sufficient rule, and consequently the scripture and ministry were set light by. They speak much for the dwelling and working of the Spirit in us, but little of justification, and the pardon of sin, and our reconciliation with God through Jesus Christ; they pretend their dependence on the Spirit's conduct, against set times of prayer and against sacraments, and against their due esteem of scripture and ministry. They will not have the scripture called the word of God. Their principal zeal lieth in railing at the ministers as hirelings, deceivers, false prophets, etc., and in refusing to swear before a magistrate, or to put off their hat to any, or to say 'you' instead of 'thou' or 'thee,' which are their words to all. At first they did use to fall into tremblings and sometimes vomitings in their meetings, and pretended to be violently acted by the Spirit: but now that is ceased, they only meet, and he that pretendeth to be moved by the Spirit speaketh; and sometimes they say nothing, but sit an hour or more in silence, and then depart. One while divers of them went naked through divers chief towns and cities of the land, as a prophetical act; some of them have famished and drowned themselves in melancholy."[1]

---

[1] *Autobiography*, bk. i. p. 77.

Baxter was writing at the end of his life, and he could contrast the comparatively ordered and demure aspect of the Quakers, whose leader was William Penn, with the demented fanaticism of the earlier time when for a brief space the unhappy James Nayler held a principal place in the sect. The barbarity which marked the action of Parliament with respect to that wretched enthusiast [1]

---

[1] The debate on Nayler's punishment is an amazing exhibition of blended fanaticism and cruelty. The final result was the following resolution:—" That James Nayler be set on the pillory, with his head in the pillory, in the New Palace, Westminster, during the space of two hours, on Thursday next, and be whipped by the hangman through the streets of Westminster to the Old Exchange, London, and there, likewise, to be set upon the pillory, with his head in the pillory, for the space of two hours, between the hours of eleven and one, on Saturday next, in each of the said places, wearing a paper containing an inscription of his crimes, and that, at the Old Exchange, his tongue shall be bored through with a hot iron, and that he be there also stigmatised in the forehead with the letter B; and that he be afterwards sent to Bristol and conveyed into and through the said city, on a horse bare ridged, with his face back and there also publickly whipped, the next market day after he comes thither, and that from thence he be committed to prison in Bridewell, London, and there restrained from the society of all people, and kept to hard labour till he be released by the Parliament: and during that time be debarred of the use of pen, ink, and paper, and have no relief but what he earns by his daily labour." This barbarous sentence was actually carried out.

v. Burton's *Cromwellian Diary*, vol. I. p. 158. There is a careful account of the unfortunate Nayler in the *Dict. of Nat. Biog.*, vol. xl.

is itself sufficient proof of panic; the discussions on Quakerism which his case induced in Parliament discover the unanimity of repugnance which possessed the House against a movement which seemed plainly anarchic in tendency and blasphemous in method. At the time men could not be blamed for thinking that stern measures were necessary for dealing with enthusiasts who, as the Lord Chief Justice declared, "openly professed against the ministers and ordinances and magistracy too." It was impossible then to foresee the rapid subsidence of that early madness, or to understand that even then its violence was much more closely connected with the severities exerted in its repression than with the principles of Quaker teaching. Alike in its initial fanaticism, in its quick relapse into secularity, in its loss of the public confidence as a religious movement, in its waxing power as a philanthropic influence, Quakerism is unique. No one will question the great services it has rendered to humanity in later times, but none can deny that its early extravagances prolonged the reign of religious intolerance. We may go farther and say that Quakerism in its early enthusiasm *could* not be tolerated by any self-respecting government. Just as Roman Catholics were properly excluded from the full enjoyments of civil rights until they had demonstrated their practical repudiation of the formal theories of their Church which were inconsistent with the security of the Constitution, so the Quakers were justly held to be unfit for toleration until they had abandoned a procedure incompatible with public order. In both cases it may not be doubted that severity provoked fanaticism, but certainly in neither was severity unexcused by fanaticism.

VII

The circumstances under which the Restoration of the Monarchy was effected might have been thought eminently favourable to the establishment of religious toleration. On all hands men were weary of strife; the shibboleths of the great controversy were generally discredited; a salutary distrust of fanaticism was widely spread. The conduct of public affairs had passed out of the hands of zealots into those of less principled and more cautious politicians, to whom compromise was easy. The actual Restoration, so far as it could be credited to any party, was the work of the Presbyterians, as they were commonly styled, who certainly included the serious Puritans of all kinds. It had been preceded by friendly negotiations between the leaders on both sides; it was carried out under pledges of liberty. The Declaration of Breda, when critically examined, is seen to be vague and elusive, but at the time was thought to be clear and decided enough. "And," so runs the paragraph on the religious question, "because the passion and uncharitableness of the times have produced several opinions in religion, by which men are engaged in parties and animosities against each other (which, when they shall hereafter unite in a freedom of conversation, will be composed or better understood) we do declare a liberty to tender consciences, and that no man shall be disquieted or called in question for differences of opinion in matter of religion, which do not disturb the peace of the kingdom, and that we shall be ready to consent to such an Act of Parliament as, upon mature deliberation, shall be offered to us, for the full granting that indulgence."

Neither the Presbyterians nor Charles II. really grasped the situation in England. The former underrated the strength of the reaction against Puritan experiments in government; the latter ignored the immense change in the whole position of parties which his return to England would effect. The Church that re-entered on possession of its ancient heritage in 1660 was, in many important respects, an altered Church.[1] Persecution may purify, but it rarely widens, and never softens those whom it affects. The Anglican exiles came back with sharpened prejudices and narrowed sympathies, but this was not all. Those years of exile had been years of unflagging controversy. There is no stronger intellectual stimulus than peril, and the peril of Anglicanism had been extreme. The ancient adversary Rome had seized the opportunity to press its claims; the arguments of the enemies of Prelacy were commended by their apparent success. Abundant evidence has survived to show that the notion was as general as it was plausible, that Anglicanism was about

---

[1] Baxter constantly affirms the change which, in his own experience, had passed over Anglicanism. Thus (*Autobiog.*, i. 207), "Since the war, the Diocesan party by Dr. Hammond's means was gone to a greater distance, and grown higher than before, and denied the very being of the reformed churches and ministry; and avoided all ways of agreement with them, but by an absolute submission to their power, as the Papists do by the Protestants." In *Gildas Salvianus* [Works, ed. Orme, vol. xiv. p. 171 f.] he writes very indignantly on the subject. "Must the people" (he asks) "turn their backs on the assemblies and ordinances of God? Is it better for them to have no preaching, and no sacraments, and no public communion in God's worship, than to have it in an assembly that hath not a prelate over it, or from a minister ordained without his consent? I confess I would not for all the world stand guilty before God of the injury that this doctrine hath already done to men's souls, much less of what it evidently tendeth to." The whole passage should be read.

to die out altogether. That expectation was disappointed. The Church displayed an amazing vitality hitherto unsuspected. A series of vigorous and able apologies made their appearance. The pens of the banished divines were ceaselessly active, and a copious literature of positive Anglicanism came into being. Cosin, Bramhall, Hammond, Thorndike, Taylor, and many others defended the Anglican position against all enemies. Their learning was considerable, their devotion admirable, their industry astonishing. The Church of England became distinctive, logical, exclusive; there really was no longer a conscientious desire on the Anglican side for the kind of comprehension which Baxter and his friends in England were counting upon.[1] Laud was a martyr and Charles I. a canonised saint. If the restored Anglicans had found them-

---

[1] Baxter ascribes the reluctance of moderate men to join Charles II. in his invasion of England, which ended in the rout at Worcester, to the implacable attitude of the prelatical divines under Hammond's influence. "It is hard to bring men readily to venture their lives to bring themselves into a prison, or beggary, or banishment" [*v. Autobiog.*, i. p. 68]. For Hammond's views see the treatises "Of Schism, a defence of the Church of England against the exceptions of the Romanists," and "A parænesis or seasonable exhortatory to all true sons of the Church of England" [*Miscellaneous Theological Works*, vol. ii., Lib. of Ang.-Cath. Theol.]. Hammond presented that combination of natural sweetness, theological sanity, and ecclesiastical intolerance which modern Anglicanism appears to foster.

selves encountered by such a national sentiment as that which had given strength to the Long Parliament, they might have moderated their ecclesiastical theory and accepted a genuine compromise with their religious rivals; but they found nothing of the kind. On the contrary, all things facilitated the intolerance to which they inclined.

The intense unpopularity of the Presbyterian discipline placed at the disposal of the hierarchy forces of public opinion which assuredly neither the bishops nor their system could have secured. There was no general feeling in favour of the Prayer-book and the bishops. The episcopal system was dear to the memory of the non-religious and irreligious masses as being the negation of any effective moral discipline; it was welcomed as promising release from an intolerable yoke. As the Cavaliers re-entered on their estates and realised the whole extent of their losses, it is not wonderful that they were filled with a vengeful resentment, which easily expressed itself in political action when opportunity came. Charles II. and his brother pursued a policy which the mass of Englishmen hated: they ran counter to the Protestant feeling of the nation.

Their experiments in toleration were determined by political exigencies, never by political principles, and, therefore, they never succeeded in gaining any serious support even from those sections of the community which had suffered most from the established system.[1] By bringing into prominence the essential agreement of the nation on the fundamental issue of Protestantism, the restored Stuarts promoted the victory of so much toleration as the circumstances of the country admitted. It was impossible to maintain the repressive system, built up under the ex-

---

[1] The intrinsic falseness of Stuart patronage of religious liberty was instinctively divined by sincere men of all parties. Anthony Wood gives a curious account of James II.'s homily on charity to the Vice-Chancellor of Oxford, during a visit to the University, plainly designed to promote the most flagrant violence to law and conscience in the interest of his Romanising crusade. The king was evidently possessed by the desire to push that project, and he showed the fact in everything he said and did. In complimenting South on his preaching, he took occasion to remark "that he heard many of them used notes in their sermons, but none of his church ever did." Mr. Clark, of All Souls, was reminded that as a fellow of that College he was "bound by statute to pray for the dead." In parting from the vice-chancellor and doctors, the king said, "I must tell you that in the king my father's time the Church of England's men and the Catholicks loved each other and were, as 'twere, all one; but now there is gotten a spirit among you which is quite contrary." The Popish plot was still fresh in the popular memory, and might justify some contempt of Protestant tolerance. But even more recent was the "Revocation of the Edict of Nantes" [1685], which cast a suggestive light on Romanist notions of religious liberty. *v.* Wood's *Life and Times*, vol. iii. p. 232 f. [Oxford Historical Society.]

asperating conditions of the Restoration, when Anglicans and Nonconformists had united in effecting the Revolution. LOCKE certainly uttered the general feeling of thoughtful Englishmen when he summed up the situation in his brief preface to *A letter concerning Toleration.*

"Our government," he said, "has not only been partial in matters of religion, but those also who have suffered under that partiality, and have therefore endeavoured by their writings to vindicate their own rights and liberties, have for the most part done it upon narrow principles, suited only to the interests of their own sects. This narrowness of spirit on all sides has undoubtedly been the principal occasion of our miseries and confusions. But whatever have been the occasions, it is now high time to seek for a thorough cure. We have need of more generous remedies than what have yet been made use of in our distemper. It is neither declarations of indulgence, nor acts of comprehension, such as have yet been practised or projected amongst us, that can do the work. The first will but palliate, the second increase our evil." Locke's ideal was "absolute liberty, just and true liberty, equal and impartial liberty"; but for that the nation was not then prepared. The Toleration Act [1689] fell far short of the philosopher's conception. Its range was limited to Protestants, and from that category all but orthodox believers were excluded. Substantially the system of the Commonwealth was incorporated in the statute, with the difference that in the interval the established Church had again become "prelatic." The exceptional situation of the Quakers was recognised in the matter of oaths and ignored in that of tithes. Property rights could not be sacrificed even to the alleged distress of conscience. Dissenting ministers were permitted to officiate in certified meeting houses, open to the public, on condition that they subscribed the Articles of Religion with exception of three Articles and part of a fourth. In the case of Anabaptists a further concession was made to cover their objection to infant baptism. Thus the Toleration Act secured a very modest instalment of that "absolute liberty" for which Locke pleaded, but its very modesty was a pledge of its practical success. The sentiment of the nation was certainly hostile to any larger measure, and remained hostile for generations. No conclusion emerges more clearly from a review of religious legislation than the practical futility of outrunning popular opinion; until the English people had become tolerant, a genuine religious equality was unattainable, and only in proportion to the actual tolerance of society can laws, the most liberal in the world, affect anything.

Even now, after more than two centuries, it would be a rash thing to affirm that the settled temper of the masses is tolerant; interest in religion has declined, and zeal is very generally discredited. Men's passions are more easily engaged in the conflicts of trade and class; we are all secularists now. It is in these altered directions of the popular interests rather than in any genuine improvement of the national temper that the security of religious liberty among us must perhaps be sought.

www.ingramcontent.com/pod-product-compliance
Lightning Source LLC
Chambersburg PA
CBHW051040160426
43193CB00010B/1011